MASTER YOUR MIND

Develop Mind Power

Master Dominick A Giacobbe

Mind Master Dominick Giacobbe reveals
the secrets of true Mind Power

AuthorHouse™
1663 Liberty Drive
Bloomington, IN 47403
www.authorhouse.com
Phone: 1-800-839-8640

© 2011 Master Dominick A Giacobbe. All rights reserved.

No part of this book may be reproduced, stored in a retrieval system, or transmitted by any means without the written permission of the author.

Published by AuthorHouse 12/19/2011

ISBN: 978-1-4678-7398-7 (sc)
ISBN: 978-1-4678-7397-0 (e)

Library of Congress Control Number: 2011960758

Any people depicted in stock imagery provided by Thinkstock are models, and such images are being used for illustrative purposes only.
Certain stock imagery © Thinkstock.

Because of the dynamic nature of the Internet, any web addresses or links contained in this book may have changed since publication and may no longer be valid. The views expressed in this work are solely those of the author and do not necessarily reflect the views of the publisher, and the publisher hereby disclaims any responsibility for them.

Dedication

This book is dedicated to Christina Giacobbe, my wife of 30 years. Christina was a victim of a traumatic brain injury and suffered severely. She was a 4th degree Black Belt in Tang Soo Do, Korean Karate. She was in top physical condition and had the mind of a scholar. She read books daily and was extremely intelligent. She was very active and a business minded person. She had an extremely high education level and could hold a conversation with the most intelligent. After the brain injury she lost total mind consciousness. At first she struggled for life as she was in a deep coma. Each organ and each function for life was affected. Her heart, liver and breathing were assisted with medications and she was on a respirator. Working with many of the top neurologist in the world to try and bring her brain back to a normal state of mind was the goal. I was seeing the effects of a body without any mind. As the lower brain functions resumed and she learned to breathe and function without life support, the nervous system was contracting the body and she was falling victim to the nerves working without any communication from the mind. This once beautiful, strong and intelligent lady was now locked in a fetal position unable to speak, hear, move or be in contact with the world. She could open her eyes but she did not see or focus on anything. The brain had been damaged and was unable to redevelop. Her face and body began to change and she no longer looked like the same person. I was now beginning to understand how the brain affected life and how the mind made us human. As a student of meditation and the practitioner of Mind Power I was seeing the complete opposite of a human without a mind. Christina had always motivated me to write books and translate knowledge to others. For her I write this book and try to teach the fundamentals for living a life with a powerful mind. She has been the inspiration for me to write this book. Each word, sentence and paragraph is written with her in mind. She will always be in my heart and in my mind. Christina passed away March 1, 2009 as a result of Anoxic brain injury.

Acknowledgements

Throughout this book I have borrowed the ideas from ancient masters of Mind Power. I thank the philosophers and scholars of the mind for their wisdom of Mind Power. I honorably appreciate them.

I have been studying and getting the benefits of the 2,000-year-old martial art of Tang Soo Do since 1968. I am deeply grateful to my teachers for their generosity in teaching and inspiring me in the art of Tang Soo Do. I personally thank Grand Master Jae Chul Shin, Grand Master Chun Sik Kim, Grand Master Hun Chul Hwang and Grand Master Ki Yun Yi. Your guidance and philosophies have inspired my life and my success in many ways. In the practice of Chi meditation I thank Grand Master Jin Lu of China.

I would like to make special mention to my family, students and friends for inspiring me to pass the knowledge and philosophies of Mind Power onto others.

I would like to give special thanks to all the Masters, Black Belts and students of the Tang Soo Karate Academy your support has deeply enhanced my creativity to write this book. I would like to thank all the members of the I.T.O. your dedication to Tang Soo Do has been the inspiring energy for me to pass the knowledge I have learned onto all interested. Special thanks to my daughter Kimberly Barsky and my sister Master Barbara Giacobbe your words of encouragement and true support is deeply appreciated. Many thanks to my son Dominick Giacobbe Jr. for your support; I personally thank Angela Mastrando for your encouragement. Special thanks to Master Don Straga your enthusiasm has encouraged me to complete the book. Special thanks to Michael Cheeseman for all the drawings and illustrations in the book. I would like to express my deepest thanks to Alessia Mastrando, Gail McDevitt and Anthony Crisafulli for editing and assisting in the literature of the book.

Working on this book has been a great sacrifice to my time and energy, I apologize to any family members, my students and my friends, who I have neglected while writing. My family has awakened my intellectual talents and inspired me to convert all the martial arts knowledge I have gained and gave me the energy to write this book.

Finally, I give my sincerest thanks and appreciation to Christina Giacobbe, my wife of 30 years, who passed away March 1, 2009, her insights, suggestions and wisdom have inspired this book to be written. She is deeply missed. I personally write this book for her.

To all the students of Tang Soo Do, I say "Ko Mop Sum Ni Da", "TANG SOO!"

INTRODUCTION

All humans are well equipped with a brain and within the brain is the mind. The mind is the thinking, feeling, sensing and remembering part of the brain; it is the part of the brain we are most familiar with. Our mind controls our every action; it is our discipline and our behavior of our daily lives. Learning to use the mind to its fullest potential and guiding it in a positive direction is the art of mind power. Through this book I will teach you how to use your mind, how to increase its potential and exercises you can do to develop a strong and powerful mind for a strong and powerful life. The art of mind power was developed thousands of years ago when monks were seeking ways of increasing their mind to reach the highest level of purity of life. They found that with a powerful mind they could stay disciplined and that was the key to becoming enlightened.

The monks would spend hours a day practicing meditation and breathing exercises to increase the power of the mind. Through this hard work comes the art of mind power. We do not have to live timid lives with fear and uncertainty. With mind power we will be confident, positive and strong willed. You will learn to be confident in your thoughts and not have any negativity in your actions. Remember you control your mind, so if you can develop it to be strong and positive, your actions will also be strong and positive.

In this book I will teach several different methods of mind training, mental exercising, meditation, breathing exercises and physical fitness, which will be the keys to mind power. Meditation is to the mind what exercise is to the body. Breathing exercises are also very important functions for mind power. We say breathing is the bridge between the spiritual mind and the functional body. If we can control, direct and develop our breathing we can then increase our strength of mind. Exercise, fitness and physical strength develops a healthy body, which is needed for a healthy brain. A healthy body is important for mind power. If your body is sick and weak you will not have the ability to develop a true powerful mind power.

It is also important to understand the brain, its functions and how it relates to the mind and the body. Education of the brain will allow you to develop your mind to its fullest potential. When we truly understand the functions of the brain we can then learn how to direct and develop it. Mind power is the brain working to its fullest potential and the ability to make healthy and productive thoughts. It is the ability to overcome the body and not allow the body to control the mind. It is overcoming pain and distractions, it is not making mistakes and not allowing failure, it is the power within the brain which is unstoppable.

Humans are the only animal which uses only ten percent of its brain. Through mind power you will increase the usage of the brain and increase the strength of the mind. You will develop a mind which will use more then ten percent of the brain, and through the increased usage of the brain you will experience new powers and new abilities. Through mind power you will increase your spiritual self and develop a sixth sense of mental power and you will learn to feel with the mind. The first step to increasing the brain usage is learning and understanding the brain functions. Once you fully understand the brain and its functions, then you can perform various exercises through the physical body and the spiritual self. The development of knowledge, breathing, relaxation, meditation, memory development, physical fitness and positive thinking, will be key tools to enhance and increase the brains working capacity. This will then expand the usage capacity of the brain and you will be on your way to becoming a true MIND MASTER.

Grand Master Dominick Giacobbe demonstrating the Power of the Mind with motorcycle spokes pierced through his arms and buckets of water hanging from the spokes. This is done with no bleeding and no Pain. Tuscany, Italy, October 2011

Grand Master D A Giacobbe, demonstrating the power of the mind laying on a bed of broken Glass with 400 pounds of cement blocks smashed on his chest with a sledge hammer. "Incredible Sunday" TV show,

Grand Master D A Giacobbe here demonstrating his mental strength by pulling a van with his teeth, Blackwood, N J, 1982

Grand Master D A Giacobbe demonstrating the amazing power of the mind, here with buckets of water hanging form motorcycles spokes pierced through his arms. Live demonstration Tuscany, Italy, 2011.

Contents

DEDICATION		v
ACKNOWLEDGEMENTS		vii
INTRODUCTION		ix
ABOUT THE AUTHOR		xvii
MASTER YOUR MIND		1
CHAPTER ONE	WHAT IS MIND POWER?	3
CHAPTER TWO	UNDERSTANDING THE BRAIN	9
CHAPTER THREE	THE MIND	25
CHAPTER FOUR	MONKS AND MIND POWER	31
CHAPTER FIVE	MARTIAL ARTS FOR MIND POWER	37
CHAPTER SIX	POSITIVE MIND FOR MIND POWER	51
CHAPTER SEVEN	MEMORIZATION FOR MIND POWER	57
CHAPTER EIGHT	RELAXATION FOR THE MIND	63
CHAPTER NINE	BREATHING EXERCISES	69
CHAPTER TEN	MEDITATION FOR TRUE MIND POWER	77
CHAPTER ELEVEN	CONCENTRATION	83
CHAPTER TWELVE	MIND POWER FOR HEALTH AND LONG LIFE	89
CHAPTER THIRTEEN	NUTRITION AND THE BRAIN	93
CHAPTER FOURTEEN	PHYSICAL FITNESS FOR MIND POWER	99
CHAPTER FIFTEEN	CONCLUSION	103

ABOUT THE AUTHOR

Master Dominick A. Giacobbe known as the "MIND MASTER" is a true Grand Master of the 2,000 year old art of Tang Soo Do, Korean Karate. Internationally known as a Mind Master, Giacobbe has been viewed by millions on the "GUINNESS WORLD RECORDS" international TV show. He was labeled on the show and in the Guinness World's Record Book as the "MIND WARRIOR", for his amazing performance of Mind over Matter. He has performed his feats of Mind over Matter hundreds of times on numerous TV programs, in magazines and at live appearances.

Grand Master Dominick A. Giacobbe the holder of an 8th Dan Black belt in the 2,000 year old art of Tang Soo Do, Korean Karate, began his studies of Karate in 1968 under Grand Master J C Shin, who is well known for teaching Karate movie star Chuck Norris. Master Shin personally trained Mr. Giacobbe.

In the late 60's and early 70's, Master Giacobbe gained a reputation as a top tournament competitor on the East Coast. Master Giacobbe also received special Tang Soo Do training for several years with Grand Master H C Hwang, son of the founder of Tang Soo Do and with Grand Master C S Kim, world famous Tang Soo Do champion. In 1974, Master Giacobbe opened the Tang Soo Karate Academy in Blackwood, New Jersey. His Academy now in Pine Hill, New Jersey is one of the largest Karate schools in the USA. In 1977 he traveled to Korea to fine tune his Art and learned the ancient techniques of Mind Power, derived from the internal Chi energy.

His skills in developing mind power through meditation and special breathing exercises has set him apart from all other Martial Artist. Master Giacobbe has appeared numerous times on TV demonstrating his unbelievable demonstrations of Tang Soo Do Mind Power, in which he pierces his arms with sharpened motorcycle spokes, hangs buckets of water and demonstrates this with no blood and no pain. He amazed audiences on Guinness World Records, Incredible Sunday, That's Incredible, Evening Magazine, Good Morning America, Sally Jessie Raphael, CNN, After Hours, Entertainment Tonight, and several other National TV Shows.

At a young age, Master Giacobbe always had a great desire for playing sports and exercising. At age 12 he began intense training in running and track. In high school he began weight training and played football, baseball and ran track. Master Giacobbe is nationally recognized as an expert in physical fitness, weight training, exercise program development and flexibility enhancement.

His expertise has been used for the training of many professional athletes. In 1980, members of the Philadelphia Eagle Football team began training with Master Giacobbe to enhance their skills in Football. In 1987, Coach Buddy Ryan assigned the entire Philadelphia Eagle defense to train off-season with Master Giacobbe.

For five years the Eagle defense was the best in the league. Mr. Giacobbe personally trained NFL stars Reggie White and Mike Quick. He was also the special physical trainer for many World Champion Boxers, working on 15 World Championship Bouts. Master Giacobbe personally trained Evander Holyfield, Pernell Whitaker and Sugar Ray Leonard for several of their Championship fights. Master Giacobbe has also appeared on the covers of 6 Martial Arts Magazines including Black Belt Magazine and Karate Kung Fu Illustrated. His expertise in Karate has been the subject of many international magazine stories. In 1985, he won a Gold Medal in Japan at the World Super People festival. Master Giacobbe amazed the Japanese judges standing atop authentic razor sharp Japanese Samurai swords without getting cut.

The Governor of New Jersey has also awarded Master Giacobbe for his Juvenile Offender Program. The program took troubled juveniles and put them in Karate training where all of the kids had positive results. In 1983, Master Giacobbe was presented the Excalibur Award from the American Cancer Society for his donation of over $600,000.00 from the Fight for Cancer National Karate Championships, which he sponsors in Atlantic City annually.

In the year 2000, Master Giacobbe was inducted into Black Belt Magazine Hall of Fame. This is the highest honor a Martial Artist can achieve. He shares this honor with Bruce Lee, Jackie Chan and Chuck

Norris. Master Dominick A. Giacobbe was inducted in as Man of the Year, 2000.

Master Giacobbe, the president of the Intercontinental Tang Soo Do Organization teaches seminars around the world. His seminars include the traditional teachings of Tang Soo Do Karate, philosophy, power meditation, Chi Breathing exercises and the Taoist meditation for healing.

Grand Master Giacobbe personally teaches all students at the Tang Soo Karate Academy in Pine Hill, New Jersey.

Grand Master D A Giacobbe here in deep concentration piercing his arms with motorcycle spokes. Tuscany, Italy, 2011.

Master Your Mind

The development of the mind all begins with establishing a strong and positive attitude. A strong attitude which will force you to believe in yourself, believe in your powers and believe in your abilities. Attitude is everything. A negative attitude will lead to a weak and unproductive mind and a positive strong attitude will open the door for a powerful and productive mind. To master your mind you must first develop a powerful attitude which will be your path to true Mind Power. I remember an old saying in my Martial Arts training, which always motivated me on my path to mind power. "You must first conquer yourself before you can conquer your enemy". What this means is that we must develop discipline, inner strength and determination of the mind to overcome our physical weaknesses. We must develop a strong attitude towards our self, an attitude of inner strength. By overcoming our self, which is the most difficult task for a human, we can then have the power to overcome our enemy. So we must develop a positive strong attitude for Mind Power. A saying which will help develop the proper attitude for a powerful mind is "Be Strong, Never Give Up and Believe". To be strong is to overcome all of our physical weaknesses and personal distractions. To never give up is to never be defeated by yourself or any other situation. Never retreat in battle and never be conquered. And the most important is to believe. Believe in your powers, believe in your strengths and believe you have a powerful mind. When you develop this attitude you will be on the path to true Mind Power.

The minds biggest distraction is our emotions. We must not allow our emotions to control our mind. Emotions such as anger, fear, jealousy, depression and sadness will distract the powerful mind and hamper the true development of mind power. If you think of the two this way it might give you a better understanding of the proper thought pattern for mind power. We should think of the mind as a Tiger, strong, aggressive, powerful, in control and fearless. We should think of our emotions as the Turtle, calm, peaceful, protected, comfortable and safe. When we think of our mind and emotions this way we will not be controlled by our emotions instead we will be controlled by our mind.

If you think of your mind as the Tiger, strong and powerful you will have the ability to establish strong, powerful and positive thoughts, which will develop into strong and positive actions. If you truly believe you are the strongest person in the world you will become the strongest person in the world. It all begins with your thoughts and your attitude. A strong mind equals a strong life. Mind Power is having strong powerful thoughts and producing strong actions. Mind Power is a mind never controlled by your emotions. Is the Tiger conquered by the Turtle? No, so your mind should never be defeated by your emotions. Use this saying in your everyday life and in your pursuit of mind power.

"BE STRONG, NEVER QUIT AND BELIEVE"

CHAPTER ONE

WHAT IS MIND POWER?

WHAT IS MIND POWER?

What is Mind Power? Mind Power is the mind working to its highest potential. It is going beyond the normal capabilities, it is the power to overcome human restrictions, it is the power of intense concentration, it is to overcome bodily pain, it is the ability to stay focused without distraction and it is the power of extreme discipline. It is the ability to have a sixth sense which enhances the ability to know things before they happen and it is the ability to feel without seeing. Mind Power is the key ingredient in learning how to Master Your Mind.

It is known that humans do not use the full potential of their brain. Through the development of Mind Power you will learn to use more of the brain and enjoy the many benefits of this power. Through the development of Mind Power we will develop the use of more of the mind and in turn use more of the brain. Mental exercise is what helps us to develop the brain to its fullest potential. If we think of a human as a car we can say the human body is the cars body, wheels and engine and the mind is the driver. A car can be in great condition with a powerful engine and beautiful looks but without a driver it will not move. The mind is what makes us work. It controls our every action and makes us who we are. When we go through life we will learn many things and have many experiences however to develop the mind to its fullest potential will enable us to enjoy life in a higher degree.

Mind Power was understood centuries ago when monks and warriors searched for methods of developing a higher degree of concentration and awareness. A monk wants Mind Power to reach enlightenment of the spirit, the warrior wants Mind Power to give him the edge in combat. When life was simple people looked within for power not to computers or easy methods of advancement. Mind Power is something that takes years to develop. It is developed through meditation, relaxation, breathing exercises, physical fitness, concentration techniques, maintaining a healthy diet and a healthy life style, free of stress and anxiety. Mind Power is a gift resulting from hard disciplined work. It is the ability to overcome pain and depression. It is being positive and having positive thoughts. It is believing in your thoughts and trusting your mind in everyway. It is your mind having complete control over your emotions.

Mind Power is the ability to separate your emotions from your actions. It is making good choices which will lead to good results. It is having a strong and positive personality and a mind which will never be conquered. The mind is controlled by you and by your thoughts, be strong and confident in your thoughts and you will be strong and confident in your actions. The mind is the strongest tool in the universe, learn to use it and you will enjoy the many benefits. Mind Power is the ability to sense things before they happen. It is having a sixth sense in life. It is the ability to communicate on a different level in life. It is the ability to trust your feelings and know when danger is present. It is the ability to feel when you are in a positive environment. Mind Power will give you the ability to be well balanced, calm, peaceful, safe, confident and comfortable.

Every human would enjoy these benefits, but how many will dedicate themselves to developing it. It will take years to develop, but you will experience life in a higher degree. You will find happiness from within through your feelings of confidence and awareness. You will not be burdened by pain and weakness, you will have strength and comfort. The mind is the road to health and happiness, if you do not use it, you will lose it. The mind will grow weak and unproductive if it is not challenged and developed. The power is within you to push yourself to develop Mind Power.

The first step to developing Mind Power is education. It is learning all about the brain and how it functions. You must first have a complete understanding of the brain and how it works. You must understand the different parts of the brain and their every function. You must believe in yourself and believe that you have the ability to develop this unique power. Once you fully understand the brain then you can begin to do the different exercises for Mind Power. In this book I will lead you through my experiences of how I developed Mind Power and how I became a Mind Master. You have the ability to Master your mind just follow me on the Journey into the Mind.

When a person develops Mind Power they also develop a sixth sense. As you may already know we have five senses, they are seeing, smelling, tasting, feeling and hearing. Through Mind Power you will be able to develop your sixth sense and you will have the ability to feel the spirit. Many monks call this developing the third eye. It is the ability to feel without touching. It is the ability to feel danger or distress before it happens. You will be able to know when a certain place is good for your spirit or if it is bad. Warriors need to feel danger before it happens so they are not surprised when confronted by the enemy.

I once had an experience which led me to fully believe in the power of the spirit. After many years of training Tang Soo Do, the art of Korean Karate and many years of practicing meditation I had an experience which reinforced my belief in mind power. One day I was driving in my car with my family on a country road in New Jersey. I had my wife and my children in the back. I was stopped at a red light and there was no traffic passing while I was waiting. The light turned green and I started to move. All of a sudden my sixth sense told me to slam on my breaks. In a flash of a second from my left side came a huge truck right through the red light. I was unable to see the truck approaching because there was a curve in the road before the traffic light. My heart stopped knowing that if I would have proceeded we all would have been dead. My wife looked at me and said how did you know the truck was coming? I told her, I didn't but I had a feeling which directed me to hit the brakes. From that time on in my life many things of this nature has happened to me. The only answer I can give is that it is the power of the mind. It is what we know as Mind Power.

To develop this power you must begin by paying attention to your inner feelings. The first feeling you must learn is to develop the feeling of being in a positive and healthy environment. When you feel your environment is comfortable it is usually a good place for you and a good place for your mind. If you feel your environment is uncomfortable then is not good for you to be there. Our outer environment is like the water in a fish tank. If the water in the fish tank is clean and pure the fish will live a healthy long life. However, if the water is dirty and unhealthy the fish will grow ill and die. Our environment is our water so we must remain in a good environment to be healthy. When we have a healthy environment our mind will function at its fullest potential. By learning to trust your feelings and spending as much of your life in a healthy positive environment will aid in developing the sixth sense, which is very important in the development of Mind Power.

Monks and students of meditation find a special place to meditate. Some monks search for years to find a special place for meditation. It is a custom to always meditate in the same place. This is because when you meditate in the same place over a long period of time you will develop a positive energy field in that room which will be a healthy environment for your mind. If you spend many hours in this energy you will feel the strong positive energy. When you are confronted with negative energy your mind will send signals to your body of discomfort. This is how the sixth sense is developed.

There were these two monks who lived in a temple; they were students learning meditation. They meditated everyday with discipline and focus. One day, the Grandmaster came to them and told them of a place, an island where they can go to experience the deepest level of meditation. He had told them that if they practiced their meditation at that location they would find enlightenment. The goal of a monk is to be enlightened so this information was what they were searching for. The two monks were fascinated that the Grandmaster told them this secret. The two monks began to prepare for their trip. They were both going separately. One monk wanted to be fully prepared. He worked on building a strong boat; he wanted all his needs for when he arrived at the island. The second monk was very anxious to get to the island. He just found some old logs tied them together, took enough food and water for a few days and was ready for his journey. The first monk told him you will fail at your journey because you do not have a strong boat for the currents and you will not have enough food and water if you do not find the island. He did not listen to the first monk and he left for his journey. The first monk continued working on building this very strong boat he was preparing all of his needs. After one year he was still preparing when he saw in the water the monk returning from his journey. Eager to hear of his failure because his lack of preparation he ran to the monk. To his surprise the returning monk was happy and content. He told the first monk I found the island and the special place of meditation. The monk could see he found enlightenment. The first monk was so worried and worked so hard on preparing that he had procrastinated and never found enlightenment. The second monk just eager to be enlightened just pursued his goal and found it. The idea of this story is do not procrastinate, set your goals and go for it. It is the only way you can be enlightened. It is the only way you can reach your dreams. So if you want to learn Mind Power, do not procrastinate work hard, set your goals and become a Mind Master.

The story teaches us that we must make changes to find new horizons. Mind Power is a change of your thoughts and actions. This change will lead to new experiences which will lead you to a better and stronger life. Our thoughts are controlled by our mind so make strong positive thoughts and trust in Mind Power. Do not procrastinate, enter the world of the Mind Power and experience the world of a Mind Master.

CHAPTER TWO

UNDERSTANDING THE BRAIN

UNDERSTANDING THE BRAIN

To develop mind power we must first understand the brain and how it functions. In this chapter I will explain the parts of the brain, each of their functions and how the brain communicates to the body. When we fully understand the brain, its parts and how it works we will then understand how we can develop it to its fullest potential. The brain is the most important organ of the human being. It communicates through the nervous system and controls all of our functions for life. It controls our breathing, moving, feeling, digestion, thinking, dreaming and our emotions. The brain needs oxygen, blood flow and sugar to function properly. This shows that proper exercise and good nutrition is the food for thought. The brain is broken into five parts, the cerebrum, the cerebellum, the brain stem, the pituitary gland and the hypothalamus. Each part of the brain has a particular function. Making sense of the brain's complexity isn't easy. What is known is that it is the organ that makes us human, giving people the capacity for art, language, science, moral judgments, and the thought process. It's also responsible for each individual's personality, memories, ideas, movements, and the ability to dream and how we see the world. But most importantly the brain controls every function for human life.

All this comes from a jellylike mass of fat and protein weighing about 3 pounds. It is, nevertheless, one of the body's largest organs; consisting of some 100 billion nerve cells that not only put together thoughts and highly coordinated physical actions, but also regulate our unconscious body processes, such as digestion, organ function and breathing. The nerve cells are called Neurons. Neurons have the amazing ability to gather and transmit electrochemical signals. They are something like the gates and wires in a computer, Neurons share the same characteristics and have the same parts as other cells but the electrochemical aspect lets them transmit signals over long distances and pass messages to each other.

MASTER YOUR MIND

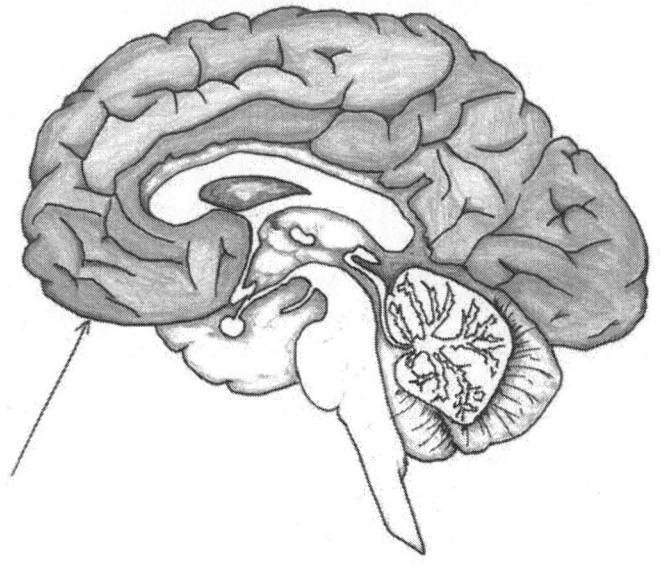

The Cerebrum

The biggest part of the brain is the cerebrum. The cerebrum makes up about eighty five percent of the brain's weight. The cerebrum is the thinking part of the brain and it controls all of our voluntary muscles functions, it controls all of our movements and when we want to do them. So we cannot walk, run, jump or do any physical function without our cerebrum.

When you're thinking, you're using your cerebrum. If you need it to solve a problem, build something or draw a picture, you need the cerebrum for all of these functions. Your memory also lives in the cerebrum, both short-term memory, what you did last night and long-term memory, a memory you may have from when you were two or three years ago. The cerebrum also helps to give you the ability to reason and to make logical decisions. The cerebrum gives you the ability to speak and convey your thoughts into words. This part of the brain by far is the most important and it is the area of the brain we are most interested in developing and increasing its use potential. We can then say the mind and the mind power of the brain is in the cerebrum.

The cerebrum has two halves, with one on either side of the head. Some scientists think that the right half helps you think about abstract things like music, colors, and shapes. The left half is said to be more analytical, helping you with math, logic, and speech. Scientists do know for sure that the right half of the cerebrum controls the left side of your body, and the left half controls the right side. This is why some humans are better at art and others are better in math. It is the increased use of one side of the cerebrum, which is common in most people.

The cerebrum is the part of the brain which is closest to the outer skull. So in head injuries this part of the brain is easily damaged. When the cerebrum is severely damaged there is loss of many of the normal functions for everyday living. Most severe head injuries result in loss of coordination and limit the ability to think, remember, speak, walk, run or function normally. Head injuries such as concussions are minor injury to the cerebrum. However, it is now known that numerous concussions will result in long term damage to thinking, remembering and in slowing of the thought process.

The cerebrum can be developed to its potential by increased exercises in your weakest points. It is known that we are stronger on one side of the cerebrum then the other, so if we concentrate on the skills we are weak in it will increase our ability to use more of the brain. For example if you are very artistic and not so good in math, by pushing your mind to develop the math which is the weaker part of your cerebrum you will increase your brain functions which will help in the development of mind power. If you are naturally good in one thing then you should work hard on developing the things you are not naturally good in. If your weakness is in reading then you should work on your reading skills. We should always work on balance and developing the cerebrum to its fullest potential. By working on our weaker points we will develop a better balance of the cerebrum.

The cerebrum also controls our memory function so we should work hard on developing a good powerful memory. In a later chapter I teach methods of developing memory. One suggestion is to stay focused and alert by using your memory at all times. Try to remember everything you experience in your day. Memory will aid in the development of your cerebrum.

The cerebrum also is responsible for our skills in sports and fitness. Do not quit at something you are not good at. Keep working at it as repetition is the key to developing skills we are not able to do. Try things you have never experienced before. For example go bowling one day, if you have never tried it before it will be extremely difficult but work at it and develop it. The more things you make your cerebrum do, the more you will be increasing that part of your brain.

The most important function of the cerebrum is thinking. So think, yes think, try to analyze everything, try to understand everything, ask questions and look up things to develop a complete understanding of everything you experience. Think of answers for every question you have. Do not be lazy with your thinking, be aggressive and develop strong thinking habits. Use your senses for thinking, use your feelings for thinking and just push yourself to think and understand. The more you think the more you use your cerebrum.

The cerebrum is the largest part of the brain so it must be developed the most. Increased use of the cerebrum will be essential in the development of mind power. I remind you that the brain must be worked to be developed and the more you use it the stronger it gets. The less you use it the weaker it gets and a weak mind will eventually fail.

Injuries to the cerebrum will be the most devastating to a human. This is because it does so many functions and it is the largest part of the brain. Nutrition or brain food is also very important in the function of thinking. In a later chapter I will explain about brain food and feeding the brain.

One important rule in the development of your brain is to do things you cannot do, discipline yourself to develop your brain, the more you do, the more you will develop the cerebrum. The development of the cerebrum is very important in the study of Mind Power.

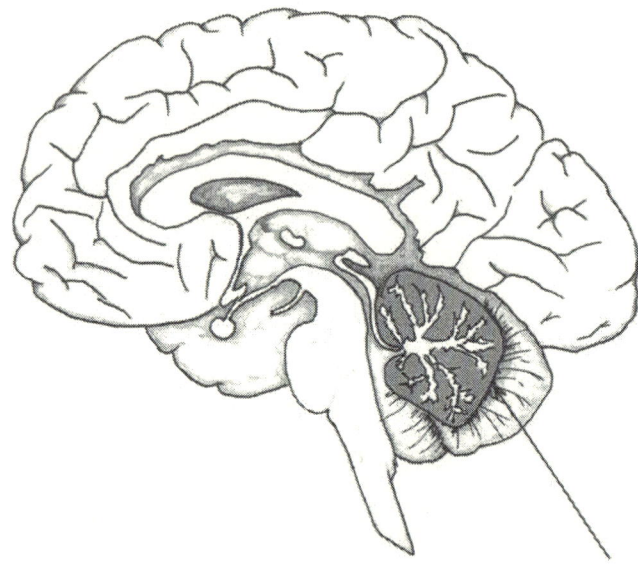

The Cerebellum

Next is the cerebellum. The cerebellum is at the back of the brain, below the cerebrum. It is a lot smaller than the cerebrum. It is about one-eighth of its size. But it is a very important part of the brain. It controls our balance, our movements, and our coordination. It is directly related to how our muscles work together. Because of our cerebellum, we can stand upright, keep our balance, and move around. It gives us the ability to play sports and do athletic exercises. The Cerebellum is the part of the brain that coordinates the body's movements and regulates the coordination. The cerebellum is important in all of our physical functions. When we work to increase our coordination and balance we will increase the usage of the cerebellum. Some people have a natural ability of coordination and balance; however through hard work and intense exercising we can develop the cerebellum and increase our coordination and balance. If we are not naturally born with this balance or coordination we can still develop it through exercising and mental focus.

Developing and working on the brain's pomposity to do things is very important, because you cannot play a sport or if you have bad balance it doesn't mean you cannot develop your brain to do these functions. By working on your balance you will develop the cerebellum. When you develop your cerebellum to work better you will then be able to do the other functions of the cerebellum better. So what I am saying is that if I had a person who could not play a sport, I could work on developing his balance, through balance exercises and from this development of the cerebellum the person would be able to make major improvements in playing the sport.

Here are a few balance exercises which will help to develop your cerebellum.

Exercise 1

Master Dom Penn, demonstrating balance exercises

Begin by standing in place. Put both hands out to your sides even with your shoulders and face both hands down with palms outward. Now lift one leg as high as your knee. Relax and focus your eyes on a spot at eye level. Stand in this position for 3 to 5 minutes. When completed, do it with the other leg up. If you have a hard time holding this position, keep trying and soon your balance will improve and you will be able to stand there without any wobble. When this becomes easy then put your hands behind your back when performing the exercise.

Exercice 2

Master Dom Penn demonstrating balance exercises

Put both hands outward as in the first exercise. Now bend forward keeping your head up looking forward and lift one leg to the rear facing straight outward. Your hands, head and one leg should all be the same level. Hold this position as long as possible. This exercise is much more difficult than the first exercise. Remember you have to be persistent to be successful in the development of your brain. Our emotions will always creep in and tell us what we cannot do and it usually leads us to failure. Learn to believe in yourself and do not be discouraged.

One of my experiences when learning the Martial Arts involved working on my balance. After I worked on my balance it seemed that many of my other abilities in my training were vastly improved. In the beginning stages of learning Martial Arts I was very eager to develop the art to its fullest potential. I always asked my teacher for things to do which could make my Tang Soo Do training better. I was young and very eager to learn. He informed me to develop strong balance, he said that if I developed strong balance everything in my Martial Arts training would become easy. I began with doing several exercises such as standing on one leg like a crane and also touching my toe with one hand while my other leg was extended in the air. However I wanted to really work on my balance and I found a great exercise. At that time my house was in a wooded area in New Jersey. Close to my house was an old train track from an abandoned train line. The track went for about a mile so one day I tried to walk on the track. To my surprise I could only walk a few steps then I would lose my balance and fall off the track. I realized my balance while moving was quite bad so every day I went to the track and walked on the track. Soon I was walking for many steps before falling off. After two or three months I could walk the entire track without falling off. What an improvement. I began to feel a strong sense of balance within myself along with an increased power of concentration. Soon after I tried to run on the track this was unbelievably difficult. I could only run three or four steps before slipping off. I kept working on the track after a year of working on the track three or four times a week I could run the entire track without falling off I had developed an unbelievable ability of balance while in motion. Soon after I found many improvements in my Martial Arts training but the biggest improvements was in my mind, I felt stronger and more confident in myself and my abilities. I now understood that the mind needs to be challenged and that with discipline and hard work the mind can go to levels beyond our imagination. Soon after this accomplishment I felt my level of Karate training had made strong improvements. I believe that the development of balance increased my mental ability and allowed me to use more of my mind. I now was beginning to understand the mind and how to develop mind power.

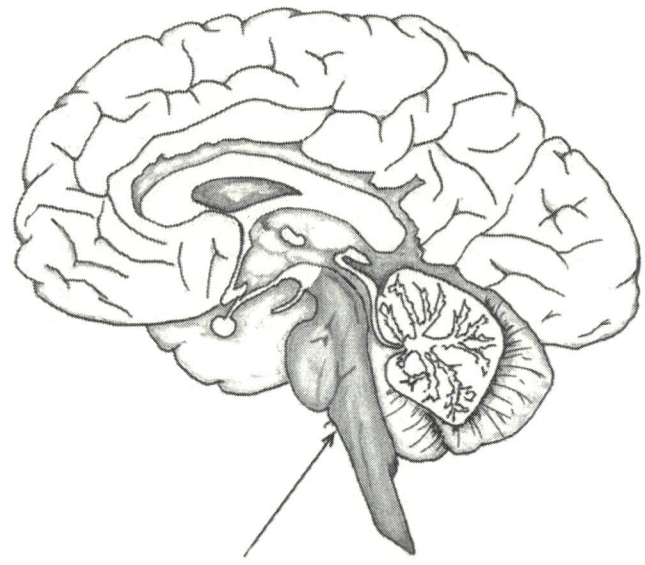

The Brain Stem

Another brain part that is small but mighty is the brain stem. The brain stem sits beneath the cerebrum and in front of the cerebellum. It connects the rest of the brain to the spinal cord, which runs down your neck and back. The brain stem is in charge of all the functions your body needs to stay alive, like breathing air, digesting food, and circulating blood.

Part of the brain stem's job is to control our involuntary functions, the functions that work automatically, without you thinking about it. There are involuntary muscles in the heart and stomach, and it is the brain stem that tells your heart to pump more blood when you are running or your stomach to start digesting your food. The brain stem also sorts through the millions of messages that the brain sends to the rest of the body and the messages the body sends to the brain. It is this very important function of back and forth communication which is needed for life. So we can say that the brain stem is the communication between the brain and the body. It is the part of the brain which keeps us alive. The most important function of the brain stem is our involuntary functions for life. The brain stem is located in a very safe place, at the lower part of the brain.

This part of the brain has very little voluntary mind input. However through meditation and breathing exercises we can control and regulate breathing patterns and slow the heart beat. Meditation will also allow the brain to body communication system to relax and give it the ability to function stronger. Involuntary functions are very hard to control and regulate. During Meditation your brain will also slow down the message system of back and forth communication which will then allow the brain stem to relax and function better. This relaxation of the brain stem will also relax the involuntary breathing patterns, slow them down and allow the regulation of the heart to also slow down and function at a healthier rate.

Although this part of the brain works involuntarily, physical exercise develops better breathing, which helps us to breath better and easier. Muscle fitness and healthy blood flow also helps this part of the brain to function better. The rule is that the healthier our body functions the better the parts of the brain will work. Because the brain stem communicates with the nerves, system physical fitness will also aid in the development of a healthy brain stem and the ability for the brain stem to carry out the daily functions will become easier and more effective.

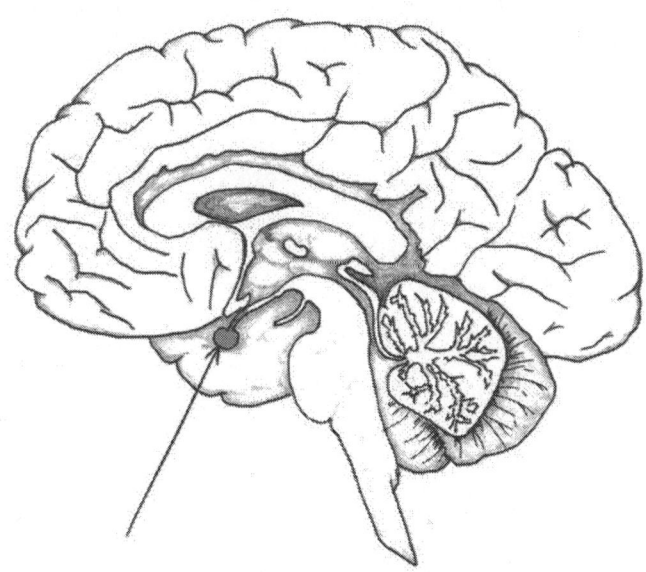

The Pituitary Gland

The pituitary gland is very small, only about the size of a pea. Its job is to produce and release hormones into your body. Your hormones are responsible for growth and development of muscles. If your clothes from last year do not fit it is because your pituitary gland released special hormones that made you grow. This gland is extremely important in puberty too. This is the time when boys' and girls' bodies go through major changes as they slowly become men and women, all thanks to hormones released by the pituitary gland. When you are young your pituitary gland is very active for growth and development. As you grow older your body will still need growth but at a much slower rate. Having a healthy pituitary gland is very important for long life.

This little gland also plays a role with lots of other hormones, like ones that control the amount of sugars and water in your body. And it helps keep your metabolism going. Your metabolism is everything that goes on in your body to keep it alive and growing and supplied with energy, like breathing, digesting food, and moving your blood around. It is when the metabolism is not working correctly we have increased or decreased body weight. Our metabolism is directly related to weight loss or weight gain.

Here again physical fitness, breathing exercises, meditation, proper relaxation and sleep will all play a major role in the development of a healthy pituitary gland. It is also known that exercise will help in the balance of the sugars in the blood. The hormones will have a much better balance if the body is healthy and strong. The pituitary gland will function much better for a healthy strong body then it could for an unhealthy weak body.

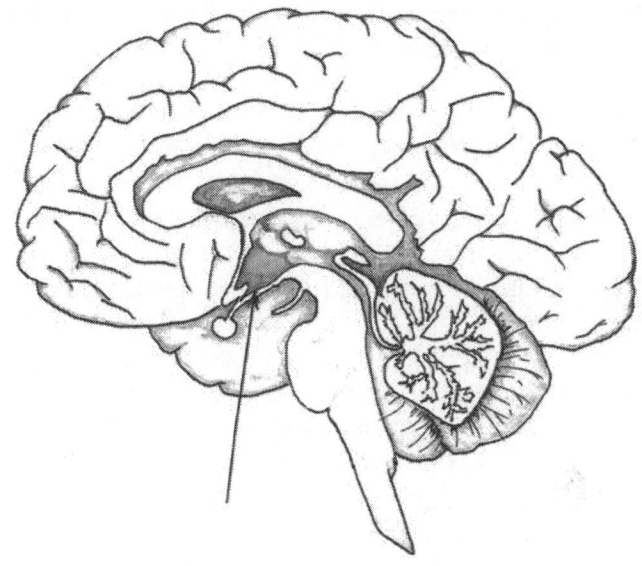

The Hypothalamus

The hypothalamus is your brain's inner thermostat. It is very small and located at the lower part of the brain close to the brain stem. It controls your body temperature. The hypothalamus knows what temperature your body should be, about 98.6° Fahrenheit or 37° Celsius. If your body is too hot, the hypothalamus tells you to sweat. If you're too cold, the hypothalamus gets you shivering. Both shivering and sweating are attempts to get your body's temperature back where it needs to be. This is a very important involuntary function if your body overheats or gets too cold you will suffer severe problems or even death. Maintaining body temperature is very important for life.

Here again when we exercise on a regular basis our body temperature will increase and the body will sweat. During intense physical fitness our body temperature will increase and cause us to sweat. Doing this on a regular basis, like 3 or 4 times a week, will help the hypothalamus to function better. The hypothalamus must be used to develop it to function at its highest level.

Another thing you can try which will help in the development of a healthy hypothalamus is when it's really cold and you are shivering. Try to use your mind to relax the muscles around your neck area, relax your shoulders and slow your breathing. Try to use your mind to warm your body; do not think of how cold it is. Simply tell yourself you are not cold. Powerful thoughts will aid in the development of mind power.

The Nerves

So the brain is the commander of the body, but it cannot do it alone. It needs the nerves, actually a lot of them. And it needs the spinal cord, which is a long bundle of nerves inside your spinal column, the vertebrae that protect it. It's the spinal cord and nerves, known as the nervous system. The nervous system allows messages to flow back and forth between the brain and the body.

If a speeding car heads out of control towards your best friend, your nerves and brain communicate so that you jump up and yell for your friend to get out of the way. If you're really good, maybe you're able to push your friend out of the way of the speeding car.

But you might wonder about these nerves, which you can't see without a microscope. What are they anyway? The nervous system is made up of millions and millions of neurons, which are microscopic cells. Each neuron has tiny branches coming off it that let it connect too many other neurons.

When you were born, your brain came with all the neurons it will ever have, but many of them were not connected to each other. When you learn things, the messages travel from one neuron to another, over and over. Eventually, the brain starts to create connections or pathways between the neurons, so things become easier and you can do them better and better.

Think back to the first time you rode a bike. Your brain had to think about pedaling, staying balanced, steering with the handlebars, watching the road, and maybe even hitting the brakes. It was really hard at first but eventually, as you got more practice, the neurons sent messages back and forth until a pathway was created in your brain. Now you can ride your bike without thinking about it because the neurons have successfully created a "bike riding" pathway.

Emotion Location

With all the other things it does, is it any surprise that the brain runs your emotions? Maybe you had a great day and you were really happy. Or your friend was very sick and you felt sad. Or somebody did something bad to you and you got really angry. Where do those feelings come from? Your brain, of course.

Your brain has a little bunch of cells on each side called the amygdale. The word amygdale is Latin for almond, and that's what this area looks like. Scientists believe that the amygdale is responsible for emotion. It's normal to feel all different kinds of emotions, good and bad. Sometimes you might feel a little sad, and other times you might feel scared, or silly, or happy.

So if we were to recap the brain and what it does we can then establish a way to make it more powerful. We can begin by saying if we could find a way to use more than ten percent of the brain our brain would become stronger and we can then develop mind power. Mind power is established when the human brain expands to fifteen or twenty percent of its potential use. In the beginning of this chapter we established that the cerebrum controls thinking and memory so if we wanted to increase this section of the brain we have to increase our ability in memory and thinking. Working on developing a stronger memory is one of the most important ways of increasing mind power. The cerebellum controls balance, coordination and movement. So to further increase the power of the mind we must perform daily exercising in balance, we must do physical exercises for coordination and establish a program which includes movement which challenges the brain. The brain stem controls breathing and other involuntary functions so if we could develop exercising which will enhance breathing and work on the communication of mind to body, we can increase use of the brain stem. Meditation is also important to develop a stronger use of the brain stem. Our pituitary gland is affected by nutrition and exercises which work on our metabolism such as cardio exercising programs. The hypothalamus controls the bodies thermostat so again exercising the body to bring on sweat will help this part of the brain to function better. The nerves can be enhanced by meditation, breathing exercises and physical fitness. Our emotions are also affected by these exercises. Meditation is especially effective for our emotion control. We can have a stronger and healthier brain if we follow a healthy life style.

MEMORY

Memory is very important for development of mind power. To develop a stronger mind you must work on your memory on a daily routine. In a later chapter I will explain in depth about memory and give exercises for developing a stronger and more accurate memory. Memory is training for

Master Dominick A Giacobbe

the mind and it is important to develop a strong memory. Training the mind is how you develop mind power. The first step to mastering mind power is increasing your memory. Try to remember by training you mind to be more aware while you are experiencing your daily life. When you learn to focus your mind and develop the ability of a strong memory you will experience increased mind power. When you drive someplace new try to look at things, make mental notes so you can return without making mistakes. When you meet somebody new work your mind to remember the person's name. Your mind has the power, but you have to keep it alert and aware. You must have a sharp mind to have a good memory. Good memory is the key to a powerful mind. Memory enhancement is an exercise for the development of mind power.

CHAPTER THREE

The Mind

THE MIND

In this chapter I will explain my views and experiences with the mind and its relationship to the brain. There are many different theories of the relationship between the mind and the brain. Some scientists believe the brain and the mind are one and other scientists believe the brain and mind are different.

The mind refers to the aspects of the brain as intellect and consciousness and also as combinations of thought, perception, memory, emotion, will and imagination, including all of the brain's conscious and unconscious functions. "Mind" is often used to refer to the thought processes of reason and the function of consciousness.

There are many theories of the mind and its function. Some of the earliest recorded works on the mind were done by Buddha, Plato, Aristotle and several ancient Greek, Indian and Islamic philosophers. Pre-scientific theories, based in theology, concentrated on the relationship between the mind and the spirit, the supernatural, divine or god-given essence of the person. Modern theories, based on scientific understanding of the brain, theorize that the mind is a product of the brain and has both conscious and unconscious aspects.

The question of which human functions actually make up the mind is also highly debated. Some argue that only the higher intellectual functions constitute the mind, such as reason and memory. In this view the emotions such as love, hate, fear and joy are more primitive or subjects of nature and should be seen as different from the mind. Others argue that the relationship to the emotional sides of the human person cannot be separated, that they are of the same nature and origin, and that they should all be considered as part of the individual mind.

In popular usage mind is often related with thought. It is that private conversation with ourselves that we carry on inside our heads. Thus we make up our minds, change our minds or are of two minds about something. One of the key factors of the mind in this sense is that it is a private sphere to which no one but the owner has access. No one else can know our mind. They can only interpret what we consciously or unconsciously communicate.

The mind can be broken into four major categories; thought, memory, imagination and consciousness. It is important to develop these categories to be confident, strong and powerful. This will lead you to a mind which can master mind power.

Thought is a mental process which allows a person to make decisions of reason and gives them the ability to deal with life effectively according to their goals, plans and desires. Thinking involves the cerebral manipulation of information, as when we form ideas, engage in problem solving, reasoning and making decisions. We control our thoughts so to master mind power we must create powerful thoughts. Our thoughts must be of confidence, power, and strength. We must eliminate the thoughts of fear, anger, greed, jealously and failure.

Memory is a person's ability to store, retain, and subsequently recall information from the mind. It is the ability to store information for both short term and long term. It is thinking and remembering your daily experiences of your entire life. So to master your mind you must remember the successes and accomplishments of your life. You should look back into your photo albums and recall memories of your childhood, the fun and happy memories. Recall all the good memories of your life on a regular basis. Eliminate the bad memories that cause pain and anger.

Imagination is the ability to process, invent or create personal situations in your mind relating to experiences of your life. One of the greatest tools of the mind is the ability to imagine. I once read a study that was taken by a physiologist who took two groups of equal gender. Group A practiced one hour a day shooting baskets from the foul line on a basketball court. Group B sat in a quiet room for one hour a day imagining shooting and making the baskets from the foul line. After a month of this routine the two groups competed with each other. Group B, the group that never took a shot on the basketball court, out shot group A, who actually shot on the court. I was very impressed with these findings. In Tang Soo Do, or Karate training we constantly use the imagination. We must imagine ourselves performing the kicks or routines. When it comes to breaking you must imagine yourself breaking the board before you do it. The study of Martial Arts is strongly based on imagination. In essence to have a powerful mind you must create a positive, successful and productive imagination of yourself and your life. This is one of the most important factors to master mind power.

Consciousness is the ability of the mind to compose active thoughts. It is the ability to be aware of your surroundings and acquaintances. It is self-awareness and the ability to perceive the relationship between oneself and one's environment. To master mind power you must have a conscious and alert mind. Consciousness can be developed and improved through practice of alertness to your surroundings, by not allowing your mind to drift and lose focus.

Through my many years of meditation, the study of Martial Arts, the development of mind power, physical fitness training and breathing exercising, I believe the mind and brain are separate, but can and do function as one. I believe the mind is the life force or the energy field of the brain. It is what makes us humans with the ability of reason, thought and feelings. It is an invisible energy field that gives the brain life. It is our consciousness, imagination, dreams and emotions. The mind is why we are humans and why we can reason, think, feel our emotions and do all the other functions other animals cannot. The mind is within the brain but not the brain. The function of the brain is to keep the human alive and to perform all the responsibilities of life, the function of the mind is to give us the ability to conceive our life and to let us know we are alive.

My wife Christina Giacobbe was a healthy strong and physically fit woman in her early 50's. She was the holder of a 4th degree black belt in Tang Soo Do, Korean Karate. She exercised daily and ate extremely healthy. She read books regularly and was very intelligent. One day she had an accident and suffered from anoxia which is the loss of oxygen to the brain. She actually died and stopped breathing for an undisclosed amount of time. Anoxia is the most severe brain injury a human can suffer from. When a human suffers from the loss of oxygen to the brain, within 8 minutes damage begins. We do not know how long Christina went without oxygen to her brain. At first she fell into a deep coma. She was on total life support. Her brain completely stopped. Through ventilation and medicines she was kept alive. She was in intensive care for 5 weeks, however her brain began to regain strength and the body began to function without support. In 8 weeks she was breathing on her own without ventilation. Her heart, liver and all the other organs were working. She was then transferred to Kessler Hospital for special neurological treatment under the care of Dr. Fellus. I kept in close contact with Dr. Fellus, one of the most highly recognized neurologists in the country. He explained the problem with anoxia and the severe nature of the injury. He explained to me that when a person stops breathing and the blood stops flowing, the brain begins to disincarnate beginning from the top of the brain, which was explained in the first chapter as the Cerebrum. As you learned in that chapter that the Cerebrum is the most important part of the brain and it controls our mind for thinking and communicating. However, the doctor still had a positive attitude and was eager to work with her. Through his methods of stimulation he got her to wake up and show progress, but she was incoherent. Unable to speak, hear or make any contact. It was terrible to see her brain was working her body but her mind was dead. She had no feelings or response to anything. Soon her body began to tighten and lock into a fetal position. Dr. Fellus explained this is the result of the nervous system operating without the mind giving it commands. I was seeing the results of a body without a mind to direct it. Her features began to change and she did not look like the same person. I could now fully understand that the body needs the brain for all of its involuntary functions of life, but it needs the mind for consciousness, thought, awareness, communication and feelings. As a student of Mind Power for more then 40 years of my life I was now experiencing the complete opposite. I remembered how my teacher always taught me to use my mind to relax and develop flexibility well Christina was doing the complete opposite. Without her mind telling the body what to do the body was taking over. Her movements were out of control and the muscles were tight and immovable. She was soon locked into a fetal position unable to move voluntarily. She would open her eyes and look in one direction. She would not respond to commands or follow any directions. She was physically alive but mentally dead. After six and a half months we decided to take her off the feeding tube for life support, Christina passed away March 1, 2009.

The mind is the most amazing device in the universe. It does so much that we can never imagine. Our mind is our personality, it is who we are. The mind needs to be preserved and treated with respect. Through Mind Power you will get a better understanding of the mind and you will learn methods of making it work better, faster and function stronger. Take it serious; the more you do to develop the mind and Mind Power the better the odds will be that you will have a healthy strong mind throughout your life.

Master Dominick A Giacobbe

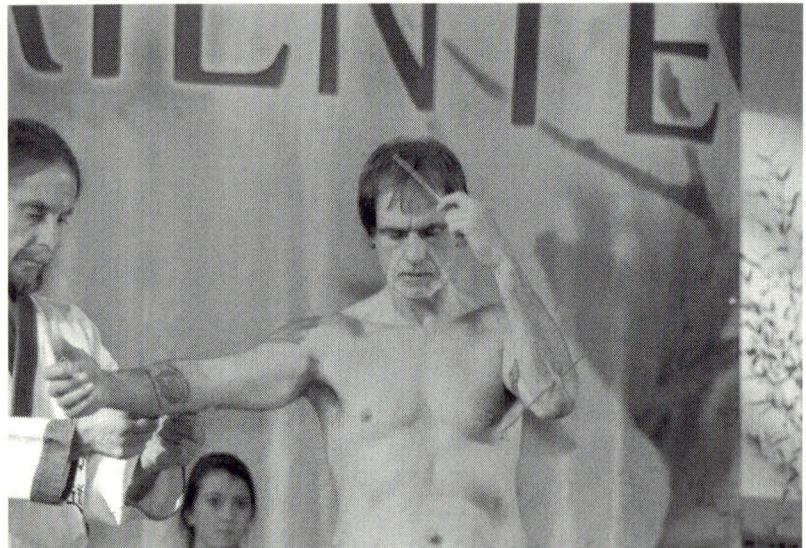

Here Grand Master D A Giacobbe is preparing his mind for piercing his arm with a motorcycle spoke. He is demonstrating the power of the mind. Tuscany, Italy, 2011

CHAPTER FOUR

MONKS AND MIND POWER

MONKS AND MIND POWER

When we think of monks we relate them to meditation. We think of Buddhist, Zen or Taoist monks spending hours a day practicing meditation. Through this intense practice the monk develops a mind of discipline and strength. When a monk meditates they either practice with a group of monks or individually. The main goal of the monk is to cleanse the mind and clear it of all the worldly thoughts. Through meditation the monk will reach a very high level of relaxation and tranquility. Catholic priest also known as monks reach the same level of meditation through meditative prayer.

I always had a fascination for meditation and the monks who practiced it. When I was eleven or twelve years old I saw a TV show about the Tibetan monks. I was amazed and felt extremely linked to them in some unexplainable way. Later in the late 1960's the Beatles explored Transandental meditation. This was my first experience with meditation. Transandental meditation uses a mantra. A mantra is a sound such as um. You simply repeat the word over and over until your mind relaxes and all thoughts leave the mind. The Buddhist monks work on clearing the mind and empting the thoughts by focusing on breathing. The Taoist monks clear the mind and work on becoming one with nature and its natural forces. Whatever the method of meditation the monks all reach a high level of mind power through meditation. It is important to understand if you want to master the mind you must practice meditation three to five times a week. Meditation is the exercise for the mind and it is the road to mind power.

If you think of the mind as a computer when we work the computer very hard and keep storing materials into it, it becomes slow and sluggish. This is the same with the mind. When our computer gets slow we run a scan and clean it out. Well this is what meditation does to the mind. It cleans it out and helps it to function on a high level. The monks say they meditate to sweep away the worldly dust. With our everyday functions in life we build dust in the mind so through meditation we can clean and refresh the mind.

In the mid 90's I brought a Taoist Grand Master from China to stay with me in the United States. His name was Grandmaster Jin Lu. Master Lu was a direct descendent of Lao Tzu the famous founder of Taoist meditation and philosophy. Master Lu taught me how to meditate the Taoist way. It was different then my previous methods which I had been practicing for some 30 years. The Taoist, believe that Chi is the life force energy. Chi is the spirit or life of a human. So when they meditate they do not sit on the floor like other monks do. They stand with their feet shoulders width apart and let their hands hang to the side of the body. Since they are meditating on becoming one with the Chi from the universe by standing the body can feel Chi all around. When you sit on the floor Chi can not go to the lower part of your body.

My first 2 or 3 sessions of meditating this way was very uncomfortable but I soon became relaxed and felt a deeper feeling of relaxation in my meditation. Master Lu said this type of meditation allows the mind to relax and become the passenger of the body instead of being the conductor of the body. By allowing the body to take over you will find true relaxation, and through meditation this will then allow the mind to function better. In this style of meditation when you reach the higher levels your body will begin to move in Tai Chi like patterns. It is really amazing your body becomes one with the energy around you and moves effortlessly. When practicing this meditation you can feel the power of the universe in your body and mind.

Master Lu a modern sage or monk had total control of himself he was always calm and displayed a sense of confidence. When in his presence you could feel his mind power. Through his many years of meditation his mind was at a much higher level then most humans. He was very knowledgeable about most subjects and this was through the power of the mind to retain and memorize your experiences of your life. He stayed with me for a year in the United States; it was one of the greatest experiences of my life.

In the late 90's a man approached me at one of my demonstrations of Mind over Matter in Atlantic City, NJ. He told me he had a grant to do a study on monks and masters of mind power. He told me he had been following me for about a year watching me perform. He said he had been to India and China studying other masters. I was very surprised with his knowledge of Mind Power. He interviewed me and found many similarities between the 6 masters he had been studying. One thing was all the masters who practiced Mind Power did regular sessions of meditation and breathing exercises. He said all the masters had extremely high resistance against sickness and disease. He also said they were trying to make a link between Mind Power and health. The monks he studied all were from different parts of the world but all had the same styles of life.

He told me that he wanted to find a link to developing resistance against Cancer, Aids and other non-curable disease.

Tibetan Monks use the meditation to develop resistance from sickness and establish good health and long life. Tibetan Buddhist tradition dictates that the cure for suffering is enlightenment, attainable through meditation. When this occurs, the body is freed from anxieties and fears. Monks know that enlightenment will bring peace and happiness. This peace and happiness is good health, strong minds and happy lives. The monks understand that mind power is a mind free to work without the worldly stresses and anxieties.

Zen Monks try to free the mind, clear it out and allow it to function at an extremely high level. The monks try to experience their Zen meditation effortlessly. The Mind Power Zen meditation develops is from the experience of meditation on the beauty within and all around you. Zen emphasizes experiential wisdom, particularly as realized in the form of meditation known as Zazen in the attainment of awakening, often simply called the path of enlightenment. As such, it de-emphasizes both theoretical knowledge and the study of religious texts in favor of direct, experiential realization through meditation. Inner knowing and Inner Experience is something that you can't be told what it is, it must be experienced.

I think we can summarize that monks of all different methods relate to meditation as the road to developing true Mind Power and success. Each monk of different relations has the same goals of increasing the mind through the study of meditation.

These are some of the many physical benefits Monks get through the study of Mind Power and meditation.
- Lower oxygen consumption
- Slower respiratory rate
- Increased blood flow
- Slower heart rate
- Deep levels of relaxation
- Greater tolerance of exercise
- A more relaxed outlook
- Lower blood pressure
- Reduction of anxiety and anxiety attacks
- Reduced muscle tension
- Better mood & behavior
- Help with chronic discomfort caused by PMS, arthritis, allergies, etc.

- Build your immune system
- Spontaneity & creativity
- Increase in feeling rejuvenated and revitalized
- Increased happiness
- Greater ability to focus
- Improved memory and perception
- Increased Mind Power
- Stronger will
- Greater tolerance to Pain

CHAPTER FIVE

MARTIAL ARTS FOR MIND POWER

MARTIAL ARTS FOR MIND POWER

To understand why Martial Arts training is a key tool in developing mind power you have to understand that Martial Arts were developed by monks. Thousands of years ago when monks practiced meditation they would spend hours a day working on their goals of mind cleansing and increasing mind power. The monks spent 8 to 10 hours a day in deep meditation. As they reached higher levels they realized that they were unable to reach the highest levels of the mind without physical exercise. The monks soon found that they were growing stronger mentally but weaker physically. As they began to learn that balance and physical fitness was a key factor to mind power, they developed the martial arts to be physically exerting, mentally challenging and spiritually motivating. The monk's purpose for developing the Martial Arts was physical fitness, mind to body relationship, memorization, challenging demands on themselves and self defense.

When a student learns martial arts they are confronted with developing a strong mind to body relationship. It is also known that oxygen to the brain is very important for its strength of mind. The food for thought is oxygen. Martial arts training is physically demanding and involves intense cardio exercising. To develop Mind Power you must be involved in a regular exercise program that stresses cardio workouts. Martial Art training is the perfect exercise for Mind Power. The memorization of forms, hyungs or katas develops strong memorization development. Flexibility and physical fitness is also established through martial arts training. There are several types of traditional Martial Arts. If you are unable to participate in a Martial Art program because it is physically demanding then try Tai Chi or Yoga as they are very good and have less intense physical training. Tai Chi movements are slow and excellent for developing strong skills in balance and coordination. Yoga is very good for flexibility and joint manipulation.

Traditional martial arts such as Tang Soo Do stress the old methods of training. When I began my studies of Tang Soo Do in 1968 I was interested for all the wrong reasons. My first inspiration was learning to fight using both hands and feet. My first lesson was a great surprise. I thought I was coordinated because I had performed many sports in high school. I felt I could learn any physical routine. However, learning Tang Soo Do was extremely difficult. The first lesson involved learning stances.

MASTER YOUR MIND

What a challenge you had to keep your back leg straight your front leg bent at 90 degrees from the floor, your hips straight, your shoulders square and your head straight. I never thought of this many things at one time. When I first observed my instructor Master J Shin, performing the kicks and movements I thought it would be easy but it was extremely hard. I was now being challenged both physically and mentally. I was some what embarrassed and felt foolish that I could not perform the movements. So I was also fighting my emotions of anger and failure. My teacher kept challenging me and would not let me rest. I was physically exhausted and mentally confused. After a two hour workout I went home upset and frustrated.

The next day I returned again and I was now learning new movements even before I had perfected the previous ones. This is the way of the Martial Arts, it is not what you think you can do, it is doing it. My teacher was not very nice. He had a bamboo stick and when I made mistakes he hit me on my legs. Not wanting to get hit was making me work harder on not making mistakes. I was learning the first lessons of mind power. Think, stay focused, use your mind and eliminate mistakes. I was now pushing my mind to work myself physically harder and stay mentally alert and mistake free. Each day that I returned I was gaining confidence and the routines were getting easier. I learned the second lesson of Martial Arts training, that repetition gains confidence. The movements I had learned in my first class were now second nature and I was gaining knowledge and performing the class mistake free. My new challenges were being able to kick high and overcoming balance problems. I would have to work several hours a day on stretching and flexibility. I was at a roadblock as I could not get my legs to stretch. I confronted my teacher and asked for some advice.

Master Shin told me I must learn to relax my mind to think soft and breathe slowly while stretching. He said when you see a deer in the forest he is relaxed and calm, when he jumps he is not tight, he is relaxed and flows with nature. You must understand nature and find the internal relaxation you have within you. I now found that the mind was very important in learning Tang Soo Do. As I worked on stretching, I thought of a calm lake of water and I practiced breathing very soft and long. I was now reaching new levels of flexibility I never imagined. It was my mind allowing me to go beyond my physical self. I had soon advanced to orange belt then green belt. I attended five classes a week and worked out at home regularly. My teacher always told me Tang Soo Do is the art of the mind you must develop your mind to master the art.

Master Dominick A Giacobbe

In 1972, Master Shin brought Master Chun Sik Kim from Korea. I was now a red belt on my way to black belt. Master Kim would now be my new teacher because Master Shin had opened a new school and would be the teacher at that school. Master Kim was very intense and powerful. His classes were extremely physical and went from two hours to two and half hours. One day I was asked to attend a demonstration with Master Kim. He asked me to break several soda and beer bottles and place them into a bucket. I did as he asked. We arrived at the site for the demonstration, first the students and I performed Karate moves and fighting. He had then made me break several boards with my kicks and chops. It was now his turn to perform and he began with a very old karate hyung then followed with some amazing board breaks. He then took out a little blanket and laid it on the floor and he had me pour the broken glass on to the blanket. He then sat on the floor crossed leg; eyes closed and began to meditate. I could feel his calmness. He sat there tranquil, clam and at peace. He then stood up performed some breathing exercises. He removed his Karate top and looked at the glass; he sat in front of it and laid his bare back on the glass. He had me place 6 large cement blocks onto his chest. Then I took a sledge hammer and smashed the blocks. After 3 or 4 hits all the blocks were smashed to ruble. He sat up and the glass was imbedded into his skin, but no cuts. I pulled the glass from his back and he stood up, the audience was amazed. After the demonstration I was convinced I wanted to learn this amazing feat.

About a week after the demonstration I asked Master Kim how he performed the feat. He told me it was the power of the mind and that if I worked on meditation and breathing I could do that one day. But he told me I was not ready for that now that I had to work on becoming a black belt and at that time I would understand better. I took his advice and continued my practice to obtain my black belt. What Master Kim informed me was that I had to first overcome my physical self and after that time I could concentrate on the mental. After I obtained my Black Belt I had began working on meditation. Each day I sat and tried to clear my mind. I read books on Zen and Buddhism. I was fascinated with the knowledge I was gaining. My understanding for the mind was growing and my mental strength was increasing.

My first step to developing mind power through Tang Soo Do was to learn karate breaking. I began first with breaking boards then cement blocks and bricks. To break these obstacles you have many feelings of fear and injury. However, with strong positive thinking and confidence in yourself and in your instructor, you attempt and succeed in these feats. When I was a 3rd degree black belt, which is about five years after 1st degree black belt, I was challenged with some extremely difficult breaks, which I was required to do. These breaks were very important if I wanted to learn and experience the power of mind over mater. My teacher asked me to break 3 cement blocks with my head. At first I was afraid of severe injury to my head and afraid I could not succeed. My teacher told me that the crown of the head was the thickest bone in the body and with proper breathing and proper technique I could perform this feat with no injury to my head. I had extreme confidence in my teacher's knowledge and in myself so I decided to attempt the feat. Before I did the head break my teacher taught me some ancient breathing exercises. These breathing exercises were to align the mind, body and spirit for the feat which I was about to attempt. After the breathing exercises I focused on the blocks and did as my teacher instructed. He advised me that I must first believe that I could perform the feat. It was the power of believing in the focus of the mind and the physical power I had developed over the past 10 years all combined together which would give me the power to perform the feat successfully. I focused, yelled and broke the cement blocks. I felt nothing to my head. I was amazed I felt like I went into a zone and my spiritual self took over.

Soon after that I was confronted with another feat of the mind. My teacher asked me to drive a spike into a board with my bare hand this was extremely difficult because the head of the nail was so small and to hit it with extreme force was very difficult. I approached this feat with the same attitude as the head break I performed in the past. I began with the breathing exercises and again it was a success. I was now understanding what my teacher was talking about as I was able to enter this zone of nothingness when I needed it. I later advanced to driving the spike through a board using my forehead. Each time I performed a feat more difficult I felt stronger mentally. My next feat was breaking a cast iron water pump handle with my bare hand. I was at a demonstration with over one thousand spectators. I took out the pump handle and showed it to the spectators. I then placed it on the floor with one end propped up on a metal block. I focused my mind on going through the pump handle. I reached my arm high above my head and hit the handle with a powerful blow. To my surprise it did not break and the spectators gasped from the sound of my hand hitting the pump handle. I took a deep breath, focused my mind. I knew I needed a perfect and powerful blow to break the handle. I reached my hand up and came down with a powerful blow and the handle broke in two pieces. It was amazing to think that you can break a cast iron pump handle with your bare hand. However I felt a strong feeling of again being in the zone of mind over body. A few years later with continued practice of breathing exercises, meditation and Tang Soo Do, I tested for my 4th degree black, which is the master level of Tang Soo Do. At that time my teacher felt I was ready for the feat of lying on broken glass. For this feat you take bottles, break them with a hammer and place all the broken glass on a small mat. I sat before the glass closed my eyes and put myself into a state of calmness. My teacher told me that we are 80 percent liquid in our body so if you can relax enough you can absorb the sharpness of the glass and not get cut. The first part of the feat was to walk bare footed on the glass. After a minute of meditation I stood before the glass and stepped on to it. At first I felt the sharpness but I quickly relaxed and put my mind in the zone of nothingness. I was now walking on the glass not feeling it at all. I stepped off the glass and lifted my foot and there were no cuts. I then took my top off and laid bare back on the glass breathing very softly and keeping my body in total relaxation. My students then put 10 cement blocks on my chest. As I laid there my student smashed the blocks with a sledge hammer. As in the past I performed the feat with no pain or no bleeding.

Now I was in full understanding of what Mind Power was all about. I felt I had reached a level of the mind most people never experience. Through the many years of meditation, breathing exercising and positive thinking I was now considered a Mind Master. The final feat I was about to accomplish was to overcome pain and learn to control bleeding. In ancient times when warriors were in battle they did not have doctors to control bleeding or drugs to control pain so these warriors learned methods of Mind Power to perform these feats. If they were injured in battle they could overcome the injury and still be successful in battle.

The feat in which I was about to perform was to pierce my arms with motorcycle spokes and hang buckets of water from the spokes. I would have to put my mind in an extremely calm state and slow my breathing to 2 or 3 breaths per minute. Before I attempted the feat I put my mind back into that zone of nothingness. When I began the feat I felt the point of the spoke on my skin. I then had to blank out the pain and I performed the feat in the mental state of nothingness. It is quite amazing that you can push motorcycle spokes through your arms and not feel pain and not bleed but it is the power of the mind. We all have powers we do not know about. Performing this feat helped me realize the potential of our minds.

It all starts with believing in the power of the mind and maintaining a strong positive thought pattern.

Another feat one of my masters performed was to pull a car with his teeth. At first I thought this feat was not very difficult. So I wanted to attempt it. It is a demonstration of the mind or inner self making the body strong and it is the mind focusing all the internal power into the physical body. I decided to attempt this feat, I took a large van hooked a rope to the bumper and placed it into my mouth. I bit down on the rope and focused my mind and began sending all my internal power to my body. At first when I began pulling nothing was happening. That was because I was pulling with my physical body. I took a brief moment, relaxed my inner self and this time I pulled from my inner self and all of a sudden the van began to move. I now learned how to use my internal power and how to put it into my physical body.

A person can reach the level of Mind Master without doing these feats. The power of the mind is developed through meditation, relaxation, breathing exercises, regular cardio exercise workouts, strong positive thought patterns and healthy eating. I perform these feats only to show the potential of the mind for my many students and followers. It is not recommended that you perform these feats to enhance your mind power.

Training in the Martial Arts is one of the strongest tools for developing true mind power. It is one of the few physical routines which will constantly challenge your mind. Karate training will bring you to a higher level of mind, body and spirit.

Master Dominick A Giacobbe

Grand Master D A Giacobbe here demonstrating his amazing abilities in the art of Tang Soo Do, Korean Karate.

MASTER YOUR MIND

Here Master Giacobbe is demonstrating his amazing breaking abilities, chopping a cast Iron water pump handle with his bare hand. Blackwood, New Jersey, 1979.

Master Dominick A Giacobbe

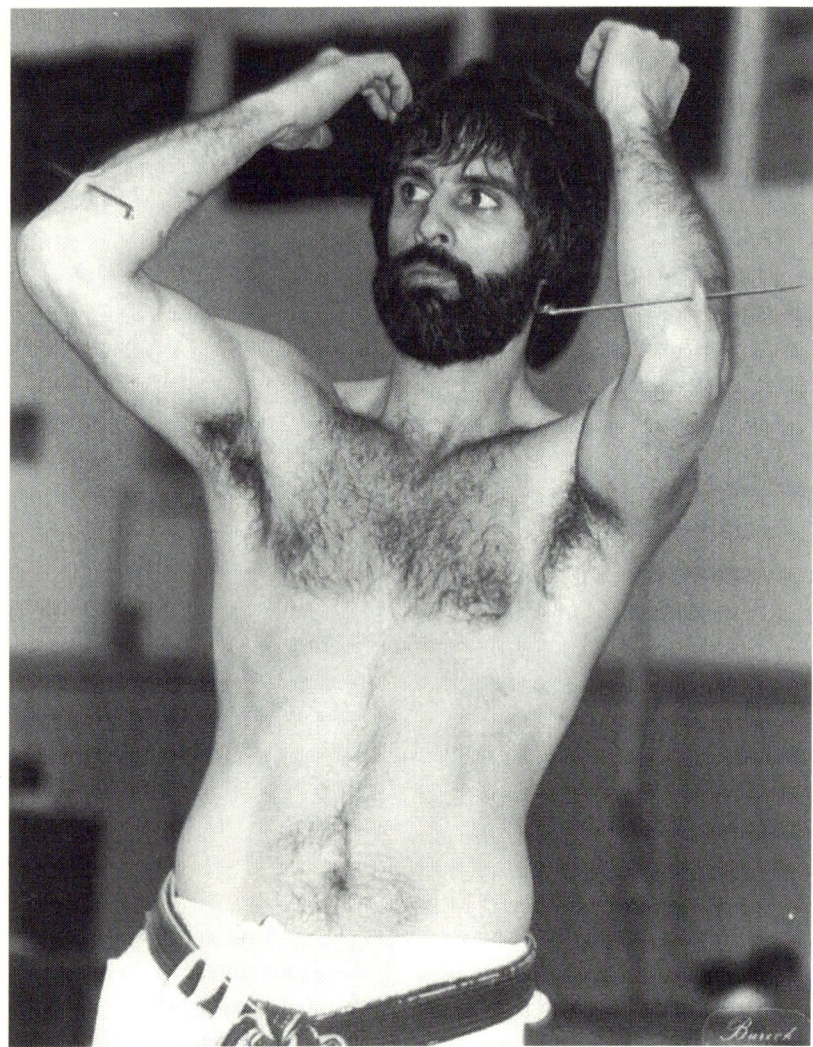

Grand Master D A Giacobbe demonstrating his Mind over Matter before 2,000 people in Atlantic City, 1982.

MASTER YOUR MIND

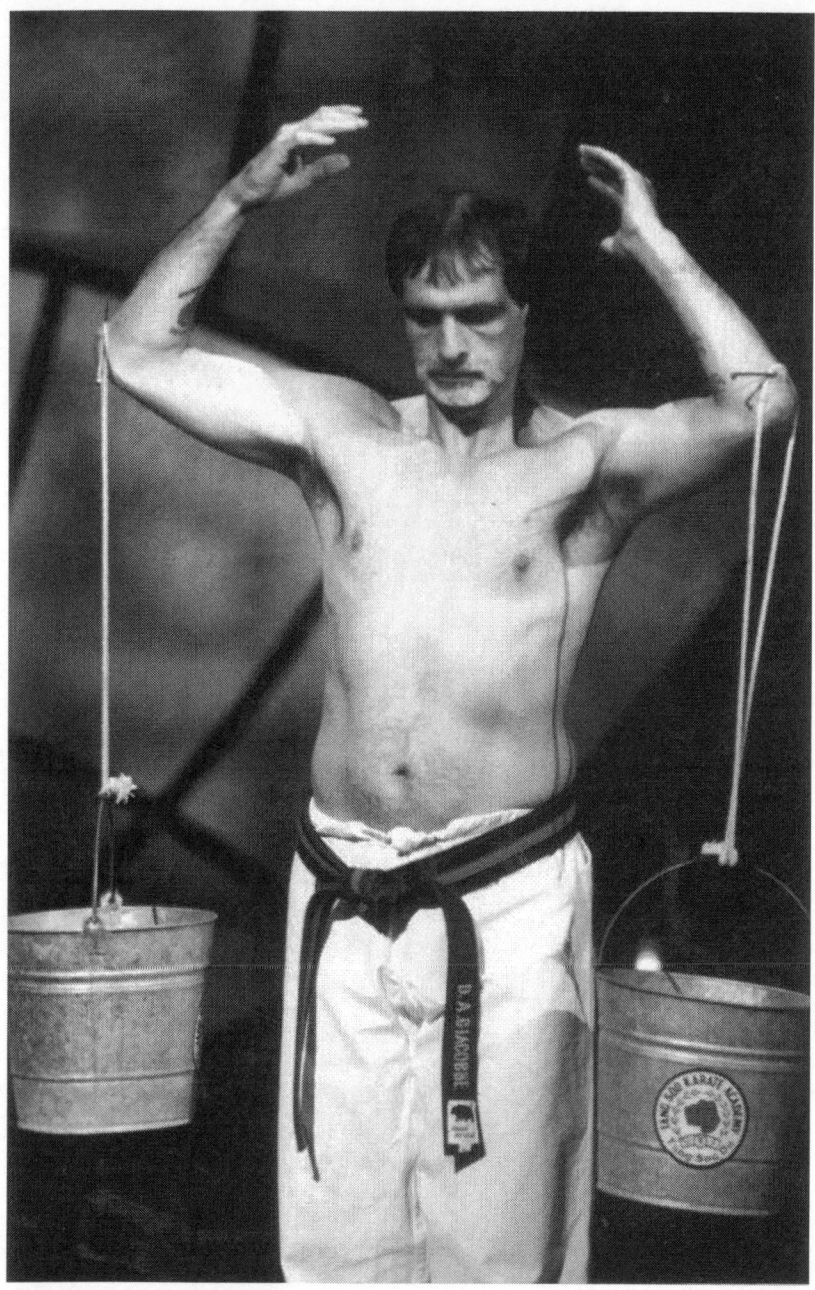

Grand Master Dominick Giacobbe performing Mind over Matter here on Guinness World Records TV show.

Master Dominick A Giacobbe

Grand Master D A Giacobbe performing a high side kick.

MASTER YOUR MIND

Grand Master D A Giacobbe doing his Mind over Matter demonstration for 18,000 people at the Philadelphia Spectrum, 1988

CHAPTER SIX

POSITIVE MIND FOR MIND POWER

POSITIVE THINKING FOR MIND POWER

Positive thinking is the key tool in Mind Power. You must have positive thoughts to have Mind Power. You must be positive in your thoughts and in your actions. We have an old saying in the Martial Arts, when you look down, you will see down. Meaning that if we have negative thoughts we will then have negative actions. So to have positive results we must have positive thoughts. The mind responds to our thoughts so if we are always positive we will then have a positive mind. Complaining and seeing the negative side of life will destroy mind power. Mind power can only be established with a total positive mind. You must learn to reestablish your thoughts to being positive. When you find your thoughts to be negative try to change what you are thinking about into a positive thought. After discipline practice you will learn to have a positive mind. Mind power is only developed with a total positive mind.

You must learn to have strong positive thoughts. For example, if you started to catch a cold the average person thinks "oh no I'm going to be sick". This is the wrong thought which you are translating to your brain. When you feel a cold coming on you should think I cannot get sick, I will not get sick. You must believe that the power of the mind can overcome sickness. When you think this way you will not get sick. The mind has the power to overcome most ailments. The same is in reverse most people feel sickness coming on and their negative thoughts help the sickness to progress. How many times have you heard of a person having Cancer for years and never knowing they had it and they were living good lives? As soon as they found out they had Cancer they got extremely sick and died. Well they were conquered by their own mind. If you speak with the American Cancer Society they will tell you the strongest cure for Cancer is positive thinking and believing that you can and will overcome Cancer.

Whatever you focus your mind on is what you will attract to yourself. Let's imagine beautiful flowers are positive thoughts and ugly weeds are negative thoughts. Just like in real life it takes work to grow beautiful flowers but weeds grow everywhere with no help at all.

With this in mind, are you planting, watering and feeding flowers, your positive thoughts, or are you spending time and effort nurturing weeds, your negative thoughts?

Keep this in mind as you go about your daily activities. Are you thinking about everything that's not right or all the things which could go wrong, or are you focusing on the good things in your life, the things you enjoy and the things which make you feel happy? The positive thoughts you create will keep you in a positive light.

Listen to yourself and you'll hear your own story. Listen to others and you will hear their story. What do you say to yourself? Do you give yourself encouragement to achieve, and support to continue whether you're doing well or not? Or do you ignore what you do well and beat yourself up for everything else?

What you say to yourself will have the greatest impact on you. You must listen to your inner voice far more than you listen to anyone or anything else. You are your own coach and you must learn to motivate yourself in a positive direction.

The inner voice you hear really depends on your past experiences and memories. If you had a good positive childhood where you were well cared for, supported and encouraged, you're likely to have a positive outlook. But if you were teased, bullied or mistreated on a regular basis, you may well have a pretty negative outlook.

Whatever your outlook is, you can change how you feel by changing your thoughts and focus in a positive direction. Here are three simple exercises which can turn your life around.

Exercise 1

Start by just watching yourself and listening to yourself and what you say. Think about how you would feel if your closest friends said the same sort of things you say to yourself. Or how they would feel or react if you said the same things to them. Would it have a positive impact, or would it have a negative impact on them? Whatever the impact you think it would have on others, it will have a similar effect on you.

You may be shocked by your discoveries during this exercise, or you may be fairly well aware of how horrible you are to yourself. Whatever the case, you now have a good starting point. Be positive to yourself and construct positive thought patterns in your mind.

Exercise 2

Now and again, spend a few minutes just thinking about the things that make you happy, exercising, going to the movies or out for a nice dinner, walking in the countryside, sitting peacefully in your garden reading a book, or going to a sports event cheering for your favorite team.

Find out what makes you feel really good and think about it for a few minutes regularly.

Notice how your mood improves as you think about something you enjoy. You can do this exercise whenever you want to feel better.

Exercise 3

Allow yourself to daydream about the things you want. Daydreams are fun and uncomplicated, and you can shape them in whatever way you want. Dream of how you would like things to be. If you find yourself focusing on what you haven't got, or the problems around getting it, remind yourself that in daydreams, things naturally sort themselves out without any effort from you.

Look for times in your day when you can daydream; when you're on the train, stuck in traffic, out walking; when you wake up or go to bed; while you're preparing food or doing housework or even instead of reading or watching TV. The great thing about daydreaming is that it doesn't require a special place or time you can easily fit it into moments when you can let your mind wander and play.

In addition to the longer-term-benefits of attracting the things you want to you by focusing on them, you will also feel the more immediate benefit of feeling happier because you're thinking about something good. Don't delay, start today, BE POSITIVE!

Positive thinking is very important for Mind Power. With the power of a positive mind you will then believe in yourself and this belief will give you a strong sense of confidence. Positive thoughts create positive actions. Mind Power is positive inner strength motivated by your thoughts.

Positive thoughts are generated by the power of believing. You must believe in yourself and believe you have the power to be positive and the ability to develop Mind Power. Believing is power when you believe in something you will get the benefits. We say being positive is the benefit of believing. In the Martial Arts we understand the power of believing. We work on techniques with imaginary situations. When we get to the point of believing that a technique will work then it works. The most successful people believe in what they are doing and that is why they are successful. So to be successful in the art of Mind Power you must believe you have the power and you must maintain a positive attitude.

When I am teaching a person how to break a board in Karate I first tell them to think for a minute. I tell them to fully believe they can do it. After a few minutes I ask them do you think you can do it. When they respond very quickly I sense there confidence and belief and when they attempt it they are successful. It is the power of believing and the power of positive thoughts combined which breaks the board. When we believe in something then we can excel in it. So to be truly successful in Mind Power you must combine the power of believing and the power of positive thoughts.

CHAPTER SEVEN

MEMORIZATION FOR MIND POWER

MEMORIZATION FOR MIND POWER

Memorization is very important in the development of Mind Power. Memorization is the key tool which exercises the brain. When we use our mind to memorize we are keeping the mind in shape. We can say it is aerobics for the brain. The more we use our memory the sharper the mind gets. It is important to constantly exercise the brain through memory training. When you have a sharp memory you have a healthy sharp mind.

Remember that special event you experienced last year or five years ago? When you think back about it, you might see flashes of a day you spent doing something special or a night you spent watching fireworks explode high in the sky. How you store those images is what we call memory. Our memory allows us to enjoy these special events over and over again. Our memories are what gives us experience and from experience we develop wisdom. I once remember an old man telling me a man with no memory is a man with no life. Our life is our memories so we must develop a strong memory so we can appreciate and enjoy our life.

What Is Memory?

When an event happens, when you learn something, or when you meet someone, your brain determines whether that information needs to be saved. If your brain determines the information is important, it places it in your memory "files." It is the ability to store, retain, and recall information. There are different types of memory; Sensory memory, Short term memory and Long term memory.

Sensory memory is the memory contained or information received immediately from a person's senses into the human brain. It is the ability to retain impressions of sensory information after the original situation has ceased. It refers to items detected by the senses which are retained temporarily in the sensory registers and which have a large capacity for unprocessed information but are only able to hold accurate images of sensory information momentarily. The sensory memory retains an exact copy of what is seen or heard. Sensory memory only lasts for a few seconds. It has unlimited capacity.

Short-Term memory is the memory which passes through the Sensory memory. Selective attention determines what information moves from sensory memory to the short-term memory. Short-Term memory is most often stored as sounds, especially in recalling words, but may be stored as images. It works basically the same as a computer's RAM (Random Access Memory) in that it provides a working space for short computations and then transfers it to other parts of the memory system or discards it. It is thought to be about seven bits in length, that is, we normally remember seven items. Short-Term memory is vulnerable to interruption or interference.

Long-Term Memory is the memory which we store. This is relatively permanent storage. Information is stored on the basis of meaning and importance.

Our brain has many different parts which are important for memory. The hippocampus is one of the more important parts of the brain that processes memories. Old information and new information, or memories, are thought to be processed and stored away in different areas of the cerebral cortex, or the "gray matter" of the brain, the largest, outermost part of the brain.

What Can Go Wrong With Memory?

As wonderful as memory is, it isn't always perfect. It's normal to occasionally forget the name of somebody you just met or where you put your shoes. And of course, everyone has forgotten something which was important.

It's also typical for people to forget more things as they grow older. Your parents or grandparents might joke about having a "senior moment." That's when they forget something.

But some memory problems are serious, such as when a person has Alzheimer's disease. Strokes, which also affect older people, are another medical problem that can affect someone's memory. A stroke is when blood doesn't get to all the parts of the brain, either because there is a blockage in the pathway, or because a blood vessel bursts.

Brain Injuries Affect Memory

Any injury to the head or brain can cause trouble with a person's memory. Some people who recover from brain injuries need to learn old things all over again, like how to talk or tie their shoes. That's why it's so important to protect your head at all times.

Amnesia is the loss of memory. It is when someone can't remember things that may have happened a short time ago. This happens sometimes, but it's not usually like you see on TV or in the movies. People rarely forget their own names and they usually get better slowly, instead of all at once because something dramatic happens.

The most common cause of amnesia is a traumatic brain injury (TBI). A TBI is caused by a severe hit to the head. Traumatic brain injuries can happen in a lot of ways and can be severe enough to cause a coma.

Car accidents, bike accidents, and falls can cause Traumatic Brain Injury's. If you've ever seen someone take a hit to the head in a National Football League game, you may have seen the player being questioned on the sidelines. The doctor may ask the person some basic questions, like what happened, where they are, and what team they're playing. Not knowing the correct answers could be the first sign of a brain injury.

Abusing alcohol or using drugs is another way to injure the brain and cause memory problems. Abusing the body with chemicals can also alter certain chemicals in the brain that actually make memories harder to recall.

Next are some exercises which will help you to develop a stronger memory and a better ability to have a good accurate memory. Memory is like physical exercise the more you practice it the stronger you will become.

MEMORY EXERCISE ONE

Begin by writing down a phone number on a piece of paper. Study the number for one full minute. Now turn the paper over for one minute and see if you can write the number. If this is no problem for you to remember the number, then shorten the time you study and increase the time before you write it. Example write a phone number on the piece of paper study it for thirty seconds turn the paper over and wait 2 minutes and see if you can remember it. When that becomes easy then shorten the time to fifteen seconds and wait four minutes before writing it. Soon you will train your mind to memorize things faster and retain them longer.

MEMORY EXERCISE TWO

Memorization of names is easy if your mind is accustomed to memory practice exercises. When you meet a person and they tell you their name, listen closely, look at the person and imagine the first letter of their name is painted on their chest. Example you meet somebody and their name is Peter, imagine the letter P is painted on his chest in a bright color; when you have to recall that persons name think of the colorful letter on his chest instead of the entire name. Practice this method every time you meet a person and soon you will never forget a person's name.

MEMORY EXERCISE THREE

Read a story from the newspaper. While reading the newspaper story try to make mental images pertaining to the story. If the story has a car try to see the color and the image of the car, if the story has flowers try to smell the flowers. If the story has a crash, try to imagine the sound. Use your five senses to imagine the story. After reading the story turn the page over and try to remember everything you read. Wait three or four minutes then turn the page over again and see how good your memory was. Reading and retaining is important for memory development.

MEMORY EXERCISE FOUR

This exercise is good for increasing your short term memory. Walk into a room scan around the room for thirty seconds. Walk out of the room and try to write down as many of the objects you can remember. Go back into the room and see how many objects you identified correctly. If it was very few walk into a different and do it again. If you do this exercise several times a day your awareness will increase and you will develop a strong short term memory. Remember concentration and memory work together. The better you can concentrate the better your memory will be.

MEMORY EXERCISE FIVE

Go back into your old photo collection and take out old pictures of yourself. Look at the pictures and try to recall the situation of when and where the picture was taken. Try to bring your mind back to the time of the picture. Look at pictures when you were a baby see if you can remember those times of your life. By looking back at old pictures you will enhance your long term memory and it will be quite enjoyable reliving older stages of your life.

Memory is one of the most important factors of our mind. Our memory is our life. Through our memory we can relive our happy moments, we can recall our loved ones who may have passed away and we can develop defenses against our tragic memories so we do not face the same tragedy again. With a great memory you will have a better life and you will have mind power.

CHAPTER EIGHT

RELAXATION FOR THE MIND

RELAXATION FOR MIND POWER

Relaxation is another very important key for Mind Power. You must have the ability to relax both mentally and physically to develop Mind Power. It is known that relaxation is extremely important for stress release. Relaxation will allow you to become calm and tranquil, which is the most important ingredient for successful meditation. To get to the deepest level of meditation you must have the ability to relax. It is believed that when the body relaxes the mind travels to its deepest depths of meditation. When the body is unable to relax it will be very difficult to meditate. Since the most important factor of Mind Power is meditation then relaxation becomes very important because it is the most important factor for meditation. Through many studies it has been documented that relaxation lowers stress levels and lowers blood pressure. High stress and high blood pressure are the main causes in heart attack and stroke. So the practice of relaxation is not only important in Mind Power but it is also important to a healthy long life.

We say that relaxation is the freeing of the Mind. When we are in total relaxation the mind is at ease and free from stress and daily responsibilities. When the mind is in that state we say it becomes free. Many meditation experts recommend freeing the mind from all the worldly restrictions. It is like a Tiger in a cage. The tiger in the cage is still strong and powerful but if you compare the tiger that is free you will see the Tiger in the cage is soft and lazy. The Tiger in the cage is unable to perform all of his natural functions for life. So when we restrict our mind and cage it up, it will become a lazy and unproductive mind. We must free our mind from the cage by practicing relaxation.

There are several methods of practicing relaxation but I feel the simplest is done by lying on the floor or on a bed. This relaxation exercise should be done for five to ten minutes per day. However, if you want to do it longer it will have a better effect on you. Begin by taking four of five deep breaths, before you lie down. Now while you are in the lying position breath very soft, close your eyes and picture a very calm thought, one which will bring serenity to your mind. Dwell on the thought for a minute or two. Now put your hands outside of your body with the palms up as this will help you to feel relaxed. Clear your mind of your worldly thoughts, do not think of work or any of your responsibilities. Breath soft through your nose only, keep your mouth closed. Now begin to pay attention to your body begin to relax wherever you feel stress or tightness. Begin to feel a tingle in the palms of your hands and allow this tingle to travel to your entire body. While breathing softly do not try to control your breathing, breath naturally. When you inhale, allow your stomach to rise up and when you exhale allow your stomach to sink down. This type of breathing will allow you to drop deeper into a state of relaxation. Calm your body, calm your mind. Now feel like you are sinking deeper and deeper into a state of deep relaxation.

Begin at your feet and try to relax each muscle working your way up your legs to your stomach, back and shoulders. Really pay attention to all the muscles in you face and neck because these are the areas where we tend to keep our stress. When you relax a muscle it will feel like it sinks down. Continue this until your body is in a total state of relaxation. Your body will feel calm and at peace. Stay in this position motionless for as long as you can. When you have completed, before jumping up, take a few deep breaths open your eyes and get up slowly. Try to appreciate the feeling and the experience. This relaxation exercise can be done everyday. From this exercise you will find a stronger tolerance to stress and anxiety.

You should practice relaxation throughout the day if you are confronted with stress or anxiety. For example, if you were to be in a situation of stress, sit down take a few breaths and relax yourself. If you are a regular practitioner of relaxation you will be able to release your stress within a few minutes. Remember you have the ability to overcome stress with relaxation. Relaxation will lead you to a happy and healthy life.

Another method of relaxation is imagery relaxation. The idea of this relaxation is to create a situation in your mind which is very relaxing and comforting. This relaxation should be very enjoyable for you to practice. I suggest that you do this relaxation technique from the seated position. Sit in a very comfortable chair in a quiet serine place. Begin by closing your eyes; now imagine a pleasant scene, a scene which you feel safe, comfortable, happy, relaxed, peaceful, restful and beautiful. Imagine the sound of water running and birds singing. Smell the order of fresh grass and the warmth of the sun. Create this beautiful and comforting place and imagine you're there enjoying yourself very much at peace with the universe. Say to yourself how relaxed you are and how you are feeling so comfortable. Try to feel the scene as if you were really there. Maybe you can imagine a place you once visited which you felt this special comfort. Each time when you do this technique you will get there faster and feel a deeper sense of relaxation. If it is stress which is causing you to not relax then imagine the stress is flowing out of your body as you go into your state of relaxation. Feel the stress leave your body. In true Mind Power there is no stress and the only way to eliminate stress is through relaxation

Another important factor in developing relaxation is balance. In Martial Arts we learn about the Yin and Yang. Yin and Yang is a balanced circle divided in two equal but opposite parts. Yin and Yang can be explained as hot and cold or up and down or night and day. We are always reminded that our life flows better when we are in balance. We must be in balance with the universe and nature. When we have balance we have relaxation. Many people have very unbalanced lives and they have difficulty relaxing. A person may work eighty hours a week and sleep thirty five hours a week. This is unbalanced and this person will never find relaxation. If you exercise you must rest, if you rest you must exercise. The closer you are to balance in your life the easier it will be to have relaxation.

The Yin and Yang teaches us about nature and as in nature we have day and we have night. We have winter and we have summer. All things in nature are balanced and all things in nature are in harmony. Yin and Yang teaches us harmony. When our life is in harmony with nature we will have a natural calmness. You should spend time each week with nature watching the birds, taking a walk in the park or forest. Sit watching a lake of water or the waves crashing in the ocean. This is nature and we must have some relationship with it to find true relaxation. We are a part of nature; however we have found a way to live separate from it rather then united with it.

I was always taught by my masters that when you understand nature you will understand life. It is all about balance and Yin and Yang. For example, if you were ever in an area where it snows when you get a really bad snow storm it is always beautiful the next day. Just like in our life, when something bad happens, something good happens to balance it out. When I have a bad day I think of my teacher saying not everyday is a sunny day. In our life we will have some good days and will have some bad days. This is balance and without balance we will not have relaxation. Try to keep your life in balance. Try to get the proper rest and do not overwork yourself. Be sure to spend time in nature and try to relate to its calmness. To find Mind Power you will have to make changes in your life. Mind Power can not be developed without relaxation. Discipline yourself to work on relaxation techniques and find ways to be calm and peaceful.

The opposite of power is calmness. To have mental power you must have mental calmness.

CHAPTER NINE

BREATHING EXERCISES

BREATHING EXERCISES

Breathing is very important for the development of mind power, but it is also the most important function for life. We can go for weeks without food, for days without water but only minutes without breathing. We say in Tang Soo Do where there's breath, there's life and where there's life there's breath. Breathing supplies oxygen to the blood for life. The brain needs oxygen to stay alive and to function properly. When we inhale the air enters our lungs, the lungs put the oxygen into the blood the blood carries the oxygen to the brain. When we decrease the oxygen in the blood the brain will cease functioning. To understand this concept then we can say that if we practiced breathing exercises to maintain a strong flow of oxygen into the blood we would be helping the brain to function better. Performing regular cardio exercising is also important for maintaining oxygen in the blood; however this is not enough, you must perform breathing exercises to enhance the body's ability to accept oxygen into the body.

Breathing exercises were performed by Martial Artists for thousands of years. They understood the importance of breathing and how it helps the brain. We have different types of breathing exercises, there is strong power breathing and soft relaxing breathing. It is important to do both types of breathing to get the full benefit. Breathing exercises can be performed throughout the day, however doing a set of morning breathing exercises will help to wake you up and get your mind functioning early.

In the development of Mind Power it is important that you practice breathing everyday. In the martial arts we say that breathing is the bridge between the mind, body and spirit. Therefore, if we can enhance the quality of our breathing we can then have a stronger bridge for communication. Breathing will give you strength and also is the key factor in relaxing.

Clinical studies have proven that oxygen, wellness, and life-span are totally dependent on proper breathing. Lung health and the quality of how it functions is a primary marker for how long you will live.

Breathing supplies over 99% of your entire oxygen and energy supply. Poor breathing is the main cause in chronic disorders such as asthma, allergies, anxiety, fatigue, depression, headaches, heart conditions, high blood pressure, sleep loss, obesity, harmful stress, poor mental clarity plus hundreds of other lesser known but equally harmful conditions. All diseases are caused by low or poor breathing quality.

The average person reaches peak respiratory function and lung capacity in their mid twenties. Then they begin to lose respiratory capacity; between 10% and 27% for every decade of life! So, unless you are doing something to maintain or improve your breathing capacity, you will decline in your general health and your life expectancy.

Optimal breathing gets you more vitality and a better quality of life. Breathing is the most important part of getting and staying healthy. Breathing is the key factor for a healthy Mind. When you practice breathing exercises on a daily basses you will gain all the benefits. Breathing is controlled by the brain, it is an involuntary function. So to enhance the quality of breathing is to strengthen the mind.

There are three methods of breathing. Power breathing is for strength. Deep breathing is for increased consumption of air into the body. Relaxed breathing is for relaxation and enhancing the chi energy of the body. All three methods of breathing are very important in the practice of Mind Power. Learning to breath correctly is also very important. Most people do not breathe correctly. The correct way of breathing is that when you inhale your stomach should increase and expand and when you exhale your stomach should decrease and sink inward. Breaths should be long going to the bottom of the stomach. Do not breathe from your chest.

Power breathing, is used to increase strength to the entire body. This breathing should be done with strength and power. Power breathing should be done first thing in the morning as soon as you wake up. Power breathing is also done at the completion of intense exercising. Power breathing at the end of exercising will bring the person back to normal breathing very quickly. When you are completely out of breath or totally exhausted from intense exercise that is the perfect time for power breathing exercises. Power breathing was developed through Martial Arts because the physical nature of the sport. What power breathing does is increase the body's ability to absorb large amounts of oxygen and it allows the oxygen to be forced into the blood in high quantities. When doing power breathing you must exert physical strength by tightening your muscles. Power breathing is not to be done relaxed or softly. Power breathing will strengthen your lungs and prepare you for an intense physical fitness routine.

Deep breathing used in Yoga, meditation, Tai Chi and Chi Gong is taking long slow breaths deep into the diaphragm. This method of breathing allows oxygen to get into the blood slowly and gently. The long deep breaths allow the oxygen to enter the blood in large amounts. In deep breathing the mind has to be relaxed and in a very calm state. Deep breathing may be done with slow body movements coordinated with the breathing. These exercises are will develop the body's ability to accept oxygen deep into the body.

Relaxed breathing is the breathing method which is a done in traditional meditation, relaxation, Yoga, Tai Chi and Chi Gong. Many gurus slow their breathing down to two breaths per minute. This method of breathing is very long, slow and very soft. This method will help relax the mind and the entire body. Relaxed breathing is also good for stress release and tension release. This breathing method will also allow large amounts of oxygen to enter the body while the body is relaxed.

It is important that you understand that all three breathing methods are very important in the development of Mind Power. There are many different methods of breathing. In the next part of this chapter I will demonstrate all three methods of breathing and lay out a pattern in which you can follow to develop Mind Power. These breathing exercises should be done on a daily basses. Please be careful because the first time performing breathing exercises you may feel dizzy or weak. If that happens sit down for a few minutes until you feel better. Once you do these exercises on a regular basis you will not feel dizzy or out of breath.

POWER BREATHING, EXERCISE ONE

The first breathing exercise is called the bear breathing exercise. As a bear it is to be done with extreme strength and power. Begin standing straight with legs in a wide stance (about two times the distance of your shoulders). This is called a side or horse stance. Bend your knees and relax the lower part of your body. Place your hands in front of your body in front of your groin area. Make you hands perform a triangle thumbs together and the two first fingers of each hand touching. Now slowly raise your hands upward in front of your body, keeping the triangle in place. While raising your hands upward, inhale through your nose only. Try to fill your stomach with as much oxygen as possible. When you fill your body completely then hold your breath as you open your arms slowly. Imagine you are pushing the oxygen into your body. When your hands come to chest high begin to exhale and tighten your stomach muscles. When exhaling be sure to breathe out through your mouth only. Continue pushing your hands downward until they return to the triangle position where you began. At the end of your exhale hold your breath again until you're ready to inhale then perform the same exercise again. This power breathing exercise should be done at least ten times for best results.

POWER BREATHING, EXERCISE TWO

The next exercise is called Eagle breathing exercise. Imagine an eagle spreading his wings. Begin this exercise again in the horse stance. Be sure that your back is straight. Place your hands in front of your body about solar plexus level. Do not touch your hands; they should be a few inches apart. Now as you open your arms as an Eagle opens his wings take a large inhale through your nose. When your arms are completely open hold your breath pushing the oxygen into your stomach. When you cannot hold your breath any longer slowly exhale through your mouth while returning your hands to the start position. At the end of the exercise again hold your breath until you have to inhale then perform the exercise again. Be sure to tighten your stomach muscles when you exhale. This power breathing exercise should be done ten times.

POWER BREATHING EXERCISE THREE

The next power breathing exercise is called the Tiger Breath. Begin in standing position with legs shoulder width apart, place your arms crossed in front of your body with your two wrists touching each other hands open palms facing your groin. Your hands should be about six inches from your groin area. As you inhale through your nose pull your arms upward to open arms position with palms upward and open. Hold breath for a few seconds then return arms back slowly, exhaling slowly through your mouth. Bring arms up quickly and take a large inhale return them slowly as you exhale. When your arms are upward arch your back and when you exhale drop your shoulders downward as you return to the start position. When you breathe in push your stomach outward and when you breathe out suck your stomach inward. This power breathing exercise should be done ten times.

POWER BREATHING EXERCISE FOUR

The next power breathing exercise is called the Wild Bore breathing exercise. This exercise is done on the floor. Kneel on the floor put your hands on the floor so you are in position on all fours. Be sure your back is parallel to the ground. Do not slouch your body down. For this exercise you will inhale through you nose and exhale through your mouth. Now very powerfully inhale strongly through your nose and push your stomach towards the ground. As soon as you are done exhale through your mouth and pull your stomach up. You must have strong stomach movements for this exercise. There is no wait between the breaths; it is to be done fast and strong. Imagine a Wild Bore ready to attack grunting at its enemy. This power breathing exercise should be done twenty times.

DEEP BREATHING EXERCISE ONE

Begin in standing position, with hands hanging down in front of your body palms of your hands are facing your legs but not touching, your legs should be shoulder width. Very slowly move your hands upward to the front of your body, while you perform a very long and slow inhale through your nose. While inhaling place your tongue on the roof of your mouth. Keep your arms up until your inhale is completed, then very slowly begin to move your hands downward as you exhale through your mouth which should be slightly open. Try to coordinate the movements of your hands with your breathing. Do not move hands faster or slower then your breaths. Try to imagine your arms are in water very relaxed with movements very fluent. When you inhale feel the breath go deep to the bottom of your stomach, and be sure to let your stomach fill and expand. When you exhale completely empty your stomach of all oxygen and allow your stomach to contract. This exercise should be done at least ten times.

DEEP BREATHING EXERCISE TWO

Begin in standing position, with hands at your side palms facing your leg. Very slowly raise your hands outward and upward while performing a very long and slow inhale through your nose. Be sure your tongue is touching the roof of your mouth while you're inhaling. Keep your arms up until you have completed your inhale then slowly bring your arms down as you exhale very slowly through your mouth, which should be slightly open. At the end of your exhale let your arms hang for a few seconds before you begin your next inhale. Be sure to move very slowly and fluently relaxing your physical body while performing this exercise. Make sure each inhale fills your stomach with oxygen and each exhale completely empties your body of oxygen. This exercise should be done ten times.

DEEP BREATHING EXERCISE THREE

Begin in standing position feet at shoulders width apart. Place hand in front of your body palms facing each other about one foot apart at the height of your solar plexus. Imagine you are holding a basket ball in front of your body. Now as you inhale through your nose open your arms very slowly to a full open position, arms straight out to the side with palms facing front. The hands should be about three feet apart. Keep your arms open until completion of your inhale. When you begin to exhale, very slowly close your arms until you get back to the staring position. Exhale through your mouth with it slightly open. Keep your arms one foot apart until you have completed your exhale. Try to perform this exercise very slowly and very softly. Be sure to relax so when your hands are one foot apart you will feel the energy field between your hands. Do this exercise ten times slowly and remember to completely fill your body with oxygen on the inhale and completely empty the oxygen on the exhale.

DEEP BREATHING EXERCISE FOUR

Begin in standing position feet shoulders width apart. Place your hands in front of your groin with palms facing each other about eight inches apart. Now slowly raise your arms outward and upward as you take a very slow inhale through your nose. Continue to raise your hands until they are completely over your head with arms straight over your head with palms facing each other about eight inches apart. When inhale is completed slowly bring your arms down as you exhale very softly through your mouth, be sure to keep your mouth slightly open. When you inhale expand your stomach and when you exhale contract your stomach. This deep breathing exercise should be done ten times very slowly.

RELAXED BREATHING EXERCISE ONE

Sleeping Bear Breathing

Begin this exercise by lying on the floor or a bed. Place your hands on your stomach with your two fingers touching two inches below your navel. Now I want you to imagine that when you inhale you are bringing clean white oxygen into your body and when you exhale you are removing grey contaminated air out of your body. Also imagine that you're breathing all the way to your feet on your inhale and take the air all the way from your feet when you exhale. Now you must try to make extremely slow breaths only two or three breaths per minute is our target. As you inhale push your stomach upward against your fingers and when your inhale is completed hold that position for as long as you can before you begin your exhale. When you exhale let your stomach completely depress until all the oxygen has left your body. Let your fingers sink into your stomach. At the end of both inhale and exhale try to extend your breaths and hold the position for as long as possible. When doing this exercise breathe completely through your nose keeping your tongue on the roof of your mouth and your lips closed. Continue this exercise twenty times, trying to relax your body and become effortless in your breaths. This exercise should be performed with your eyes closed for maximum relaxation.

RELAXED BREATHING EXERCISE TWO

Seated Lotus Breathing

Sit with your legs crossed in Lotus position. Place your hands on your lap with your thumbs resting on your stomach about two inches below your navel. You can rest your back against a wall or another object if this is more comfortable for you. Begin with a soft and slow inhale allowing your stomach to expand feel your stomach pushing against your thumbs. When you have completed your inhale relax a few seconds then begin your exhale. Feeling your thumbs sink into your stomach; breathe completely through your nose for your inhale and exhale. When you inhale fill your entire body with clean white oxygen. When you exhale remove all the grey used air from your body. Do this exercise twenty times and be sure to be relaxed and very comfortable.

RELAXED BREATHING EXERCISE THREE

Hugging the Tree Breathing

Begin standing in wide horse stance position. Bend your knees so your body is low to the ground. Place your hands in front of your body as if you are hugging a tree. Be sure that your hands are in front of your body open with palms facing your body, your fingers separated and the two hands should be two or three inches from the each other. While in this position focus your mind on the lower stomach area. Breathe slowly through your nose only. When you inhale expand your lower stomach. When you exhale, contract your lower stomach. This breathing should be done very slow and soft. This exercise can be done with eyes closed. This should be done for five minutes for maximum benefits.

CHAPTER TEN

MEDITATION FOR TRUE MIND POWER

MEDITATION FOR TRUE MIND POWER

If I were to say what is the most important thing you can do to develop Mind Power I would say it is to meditate. Meditation is for the mind what exercise is for the body. It allows the brain to function at its highest level. It makes our mind strong and powerful. You cannot develop Mind Power without meditation. If you want a strong and powerful mind you must meditate.

There are several different types of meditation you can do. In this chapter I will explain the types of meditation I feel which are the most beneficial to developing Mind Power. You should try the different types and pick the type of meditation which you feel most comfortable with. I tell my students, meditation is like doing push ups, when you begin doing them they are hard to do and you will feel uncomfortable. However when you do push ups everyday they will become easy and you will be able to do them effortlessly. Meditation is the same in the beginning you will feel uncomfortable and awkward but after continued practice you will find enjoyment and relaxation.

While performing meditation you must use the techniques of breathing and relaxation which you learned in previous chapters. I do not want you to think about breathing technique when you are meditating. It will not allow you to free your mind and you will feel like you are working. You should practice the breathing and relaxation exercises so you can do them without thinking about it. The less you have to think about when doing meditation the more successful you will be. Learning meditation will take dedication and discipline. You must be dedicated to keep working at it and you must have the discipline to keep doing it on a regular basis.

Meditation should be practiced three to four times a week for twenty to forty minutes per session. Remember it is not the how much you meditate it is the quality of your meditation which will lead you to Mind Power. You have to find what time of day is best for you. Some people like meditating in the morning others have different times and you need to discover what suits you the best. The place where you meditate is also very important. You need a place which is quiet and has a feeling of serenity. It needs to be a place where you will not be interrupted or surprised. You should always try to meditate in the same place. By meditating in the same place you will develop an energy field which will help lead you into deeper meditation.

I enjoy meditating first thing in the morning. I believe there is more energy in the morning and I feel as if I get more of a benefit. One of my meditation masters told me listen to the birds how they sing in the morning and at the end of the day they become quiet. This is because they are responding to nature's energy which there is an abundance of in the morning. Helping me to understand that to follow nature is very important, I decided to do my meditation in the morning. However you must follow what is best for you and what will help you to find relaxation in your meditation.

The main objective of meditation is to clear the mind of thoughts. This will be difficult in the beginning because when you close your eyes in a quiet place your mind will want to generate thoughts. Imaging and imagination will help to eliminate thoughts. I tell my students to begin with developing a picture of a calm lake of water. It could be a place you once visited or it could be a picture you are familiar with. You must begin with making a mental image of the picture. Imagine you are there feeling nature, smelling the flowers and hearing nature. Many times I instruct people to create this mental image for a week or two before actually meditating. This is a very important thing to do before you start.

I practice two styles of meditation which I believe is the best for enhancing Mind Power. One style is seated and the other is standing. Buddhist and Zen monks sit in the Lotus position with their legs crossed. Taoist monks meditate standing up. Most seated positions are very strict and disciplined. I do not think this is the best way to start. I tell people to sit on the ground with a pad under them for comfort. I also suggest that you lean your back against a wall or chair. I also recommend that you keep your legs straight in the beginning and later cross them. The more comfortable you are the easier it will be to meditate.

Seated meditation, sit relaxed on the floor with your legs straight and slightly open. Place your hands with the palms down on your legs. Keep your back as straight as possible. Next create the image of the lake of water. Now imagine you are a leaf floating on the lake and you are part of nature. Think of all the comforting sounds and allow yourself to relax. To prevent thoughts from entering your mind you will create a humming sound to quiet your mind. On each exhale make a soft humming sound, a very quite sound. We make the sound on the exhale because it is believed that all your thoughts enter your mind on your exhale. Breathe softly and try to bring yourself into a very calm state of mind. Continue to make the humming sound quieter and quieter until there is no sound at all coming out of your mouth but the sound is still in your mind.

Now in your imaginary picture imagine you are a leaf on the lake of water, imagine you are sinking deeper and deeper into a state of complete relaxation and calmness. Keep feeling like you are going down. Now begin the relaxation of your physical body. Begin in your face and head relax all the facial muscles around your eyes, your cheeks and down your neck. Now relax your shoulders and down your arms. As you get to your hands feel the weight of your hands on your legs. They should feel like they are pressing on your legs. Keep thinking you are sinking deeper and deeper. Continue the muscle relaxation down your chest, your stomach and down your legs. Pay attention to any tingles in your body these are signs of deep relaxation. Feel the relaxation to your feet and toes. Now you will be in a complete state of deep relaxation. Continue the hum in your mind. If a thought enters your mind try to drown it out with the sound of the hum.

Take your time and be sure to remember all the feelings and experiences you are having as this will help you to return to a deeper meditation your next practice. Throughout your meditation continue to feel like you are sinking deeper and deeper into a deep state of relaxed meditation. Continue for about fifteen or twenty minutes. When you feel you are completed do not jump up. Imagine you are climbing a hill moving upward out of your deep state of meditation. Come out of your meditation slowly. When you feel you are all the way back just open your eyes and do not move for a minute or two. Try to feel your body and how relaxed you are. It may take you two or three times to begin to feel the relaxation but be persistent and use your determination to feel the meditation.

As you get better at your meditation you can cross your legs and sit without leaning on a wall. You can also remove the hum sound as you find fewer thoughts entering your mind. The goal is to have complete nothingness from your mind. When you can remove the sound, your relaxation is now entering your mind and you are now building the power of your mind. The only way you can strengthen your mind is through meditation so keep working hard at it. In a short time you will begin to feel the benefits. Some of the benefits are better memory, deeper sleep, stronger focus and concentration, less stress and a happier state of mind.

Standing meditation is very unique. It has been practiced by the Taoists monks for thousands of years. The Taoists believe in the spiritual energy of "Chi". Chi is the life energy in humans and in all living things. The world is composed of hundreds of Chi fields. The Taoists believe Chi is present everywhere in nature. They meditate standing because they are trying to become one with the Chi energy of the universe. By standing you are allowing the Chi to be all around your body. By relaxing and becoming one with this energy you will get many health benefits from the universe. In this meditation you are not restricted to staying motionless. The Taoists believe nothing in the universe stands still, so to go to the deepest state of mediation you must relax and move with the currents of the world.

While performing this meditation you may move your arms in different ways. It is common to do Tai Chi like movements as you reach deep levels of Taoists meditation. These movements will be very slow and soft. This style of meditation is also known as Chi Dao. The word Tao and Dao are the same. It is used in both ways but it is the same word. The main objective in this meditation is relaxation and communication with the world around you. This style of meditation may take a little longer because you will not feel comfortable standing while meditating.

Begin with legs shoulders width. Relax you body beginning from your face and working your way down as you did with the traditional meditation. Repeat to yourself, RELAX, RELEASE AND LET GO. Relax your physical body, release your internal energy or your Chi and let go of yourself. Let go of all your stress and worldly chains, free yourself. In life, our mind is the driver, as it always wants to be in control. In this meditation your mind must let go and become the passenger. Your mind must follow your body into relaxation. By letting go you will go into a deep meditation. If you feel your arms wanting to lift, let them if they feel like moving in a pattern let them. Just keep repeating to yourself relax, release and let go.

I practiced the traditional meditation for twenty five years before I experienced the Taoists meditation. I practice both styles and I believe they compliment each other. However, in the beginning I feel you should start with the traditional meditation and when you can feel the meditation then add the Taoists method. This method is harder and will take longer before you feel the benefits. As I said in the beginning of this chapter to develop Mind Power you must meditate. It is the exercise for the mind. Your mind will grow with meditation and you will reap the benefits.

CHAPTER ELEVEN

CONCENTRATION

CONCENTRATION

Concentration is the ability to focus the mind. It is to focus on the task at hand and eliminate distractions. It is a meditation without closing the eyes. It is to direct the minds thought process into one strong and positive direction. In sports it is called in the zone. It is the ability to become one between the mind and the body and not be distracted by outer occurrences. Concentration is very important in the development of mind power. When you develop strong concentration techniques you will develop true mind power.

Concentration has been defined as "the ability to direct one's thinking into whatever direction one would intend". It is the ability to say focused on the task at hand.

We all have the ability to concentrate. At times our concentration may be distracted and our thoughts become scattered, and our minds race from one thought to another. To deal with such times, you need to learn and practice concentration skills and strategies. To concentrate, you have to learn the skill of concentration, and as with any skill this means practice repeated day after day until we achieve enough improvement to feel that you can concentrate with confidence when you need to. These are the factors which affect concentration.

You need to make a personal commitment to develop concentration. You must apply the effort needed to do the task at hand in the way which you realistically plan to do it. Without serious effort and a concentrated commitment you will not be successful in your concentration efforts.

You must have enthusiasm for concentration. If you are interested in the task at hand and you enjoy doing it, then you will find it easy to motivate yourself to concentrate. Without enthusiasm you will become distracted and lose concentration.

You need to have the skill of knowing how to do something. This gives us confidence which assures us that our efforts will be successful, so you don't have to deal with anxiety about the task at hand. Anxiety destroys concentration.

You must be in a positive emotional and physical state of mind. When you are in good physical condition, feeling rested, relaxed and comfortable and our emotions are calm and peaceful, then you tend to be positive about things. This in turn raises our self-esteem, which makes us more able to concentrate.

Our psychological state of mind is very important for successful concentration. The mind must be calm and not in a distracted state. If you are in a distracted state of mind your thoughts will be scattered and pre-occupied, leaving little mental space for concentration.

Our environment will also have a strong influence on our concentration abilities. It is much more difficult to concentrate if our surroundings keep distracting and intruding on our awareness. Too much noise, too hot or too cold, the furniture is uncomfortable or the people around us are stressing out. These environmental distractions will not allow us to concentrate.

Concentration span is the time you can concentrate on a specific task at hand before your thoughts wander. In learning concentration skills, you should aim to extend your concentration span bearing in mind that you will have a different span for different tasks. Most people find their level for most tasks around an hour, but for some people and some tasks it will just be a few minutes, while for others it might be two or three hours. With continued practice on concentration exercises you will learn to increase your concentration span.

The main obstacles which decrease our concentration span are boredom, anxiety and day-dreaming. However, by improving our concentration skills you will not be burdened by these distractions. The following two skills are basic to concentration. If you want to improve your concentration, start by practicing them. They will be followed by further strategies and exercises which will develop your skills of true concentration.

STOP! This sounds very simple, but it works. When you notice your thoughts wandering, say to yourself STOP! Then gently bring your attention back to where you want it to be. Each time it wanders bring it back. To begin with, this could be several times a minute. But each time, say STOP! And then re-focus. Don't waste energy trying to keep thoughts out of your mind, just put the effort into STOP! And re-focus.

FOCUSED ATTENTION! This is about maintaining concentration and not giving in to distractions. It could be described as tunnel-vision, or as being focused. It is the ability to maintain your concentration on what is in front of you. Do not allow outer distractions to break or interfere with your concentration. You must use your mind to hone out or ignore what is not important. You must stay focused and keep your sole attention on the task at hand.

Here are some other specific problems which may distract your concentration. It is important to remember that you control your thoughts and your thoughts control your concentration. Concentrate on controlling and focusing your thoughts to the task at hand.

When you have been concentrating well but your brain now feels saturated, take a short break and try to recharge your mental batteries. You may try to review what you have done so far and see if this helps you. You may consider switching to a new topic. However, if you feel too tired to restart after a short break, just stop.

Day-dreaming, do not allow your mind to day dream focus your thoughts and keep your mind on the subject at hand. If you are still having a problem with day dreaming then use the stop technique.

The root of successful concentration is having a strong positive mind. Do not allow any negative thoughts to enter your mind. Remember negative thoughts equal negative results. Be strong and maintain only positive thoughts.

Concentration should never be vague. If you are not quite sure what you are supposed to be doing or why you are doing it then it will be difficult to maintain concentration. You could try to define the task in terms of its content and purpose, and then to make a realistic effort to make your task important.

Feeling overwhelmed by our task at hand. Sometimes what you are doing is just too much for your mind to handle. When you think about it, it is too huge a task to contemplate and your feelings of inadequacy take over. This will contribute to losing concentration. In these circumstances, try breaking the task up into smaller parts that feel manageable.

These three concentration exercises will help you to develop strong concentration. It is important that you do these exercises daily and push your mind to be focused at the task you are doing. Concentration is very important for the development of Mind Power.

EXERCISE 1

Take one page out of the newspaper read it completely. While reading develop an imagination of what you are reading. Stay focused on the subject. Create a mental image of the story at hand. Do not read to fast, this is concentrated reading emphasizing on quality not quantity. While reading the story make sure you stay focused on the subject, do not allow your mind to drift from the subject. After reading the entire page, turn the page over and see if you can remember what you have read. If you have good concentration you will remember the entire page. See if you can fully remember each story. If you have trouble remembering the stories then you must read the page again. Continue this exercise each day until you can read the page and remember the entire page. Each day read a different section. By changing sections you will see subjects you enjoy will be easier to retain. Performing this exercise on a daily basis will increase your ability to concentrate while reading. This exercise will help students in school to understand what they are reading. This is an active concentration for staying focused.

EXERCISE 2

Begin by sitting in a cross leg meditation position facing a wall. Sitting about 2 feet from the wall make a dot on the wall at your eye level. Sit in that position and concentrate on the dot. Sit quietly and blank out all thoughts and distractions. Work on focusing your mind to the dot, become one with the dot. Do not move your eyes from the dot, stay focused. Try to do this exercise for 10 to 15 minutes a day. Each day you do this exercise move a little further away from the wall. Soon you will be able to focus your mind on the dot from the other side of the room. This is a great exercise to develop concentration. While concentrating on the dot repeat to yourself, Be Strong! On your inhale think "Be" and on your exhale think "Strong". Do not allow any other thoughts to enter you mind. If a thought enters your mind drown it out with the thought of "Be Strong". This is a very old technique for developing concentration. By moving further from the wall you will also develop strong focus abilities. Remember to stay focused to the dot and do not be distracted. This concentration exercise was used by the Japanese archery warriors. While riding a horse at top speed the Japanese Archer turns to the side position and shoots at a target while in motion and hits the bull's eye. This is one of the hardest tasks for an Archer to be able to hit a bull's eye while bouncing on a moving horse. This can only be done from focused concentration.

EXERCISE 3

Take a candle and place it on a small table or chair. Sit on the floor with the candle at eye level. Sit with your legs in a crossed leg meditation position. Now light the candle and concentrate on the fire. Concentrate so you only see the fire. Soon everything around the fire will blank out. Become one with the fire. Stay focused on the fire. Calm your mind by thinking "Relax", "Relax" and "Relax" on each exhale. Continue to repeat this in your mind as you focus on the candle fire. If other thoughts enter your mind blank them out by concentrating and repeating "Relax" "Relax" and "Relax". Say the word in your mind very soft and quietly. Do this exercise for 10 to 15 minutes a day. Soon you will go into a deep state of concentration. Keep your eyes focused on the fire. This method of concentration was used by warriors of ancient times. They understood that when in battle they needed strong concentration of the mind. It is believed that by doing this concentration exercise you will develop high quality on intense concentration.

EXERCISE 4

Develop concentration through intense physical training. There are many ways you can do this but the goal is to do an intense or vigorous exercise routine with the goal to bring your body to exhaustion, when your body begins to send signals to your mind to stop, don't stop! Continue the exercise while focusing your mind on not stopping. Make sure you push yourself not to stop. You can do this while running or while on the stair climber. In Martial Arts training students reach this point on a regular basis. Martial Arts students are unable to stop while drilling in class so students develop strong concentration through vigorous Martial Arts exercises. When you feel your body beginning to weaken focus your mind and send strong thoughts to your mind that you are not stopping. Focus your eyes on a spot and breath deep. Concentrate on your breathing because the breathing is the bridge between the mind and the body. Use your mind, be determined but do not stop. As your concentration develops your physical strength will increase and this is what we call mind to body training

These exercises have been used for thousands of years by Martial Artists, for development of concentration for martial arts practice. Always stay focused, be persistent and disciplined in your exercise. If at first you find these exercises difficult just continue to practice them and you will soon feel comfortable. In a short time, you will feel the strength of your concentration increase which will be developed from these concentration exercises.

CHAPTER TWELVE

MIND POWER for Health and Long Life

MIND POWER for Health and Long Life

If we wanted to summarize how to develop Mind Power we can say we need to meditate three to four times a week, we must be involved in a cardio exercise routine which challenges the mind, such as Martial Arts, dance or aerobics, we must do our breathing exercises daily, we must eat a healthy diet, be positive in all of our thoughts and have a relaxed state of mind. We must also work on our memorization and mental focus. Just because we grow old it does not mean we should stop working the mind.

The mind has the power to overcome many of the body's disorders. You must learn to use your mind to overcome illness when confronted with it. When you feel sickness coming on, you must use your mind and believe you will not get sick. You must create positive thoughts to combat whatever illness you are confronted with. It is known that the power of the mind can overcome Cancer. It can heal people from illnesses which have no cure. The mind is the most powerful object in the universe. It can do more then any computer or any machine. The power of the mind is within you and within your brain. Learn to use your mind through positive thoughts and belief in Mind Power. You can conquer any illness with Mind Power if you believe you can.

I believe that several mental problems develop when the human stops challenging the mind. Increased health problems and decreased mental awareness develops when the mind is not challenged. When people grow old and unhealthy these problems will accrue. The older unhealthy body combined with unhealthy blood flow will supply less oxygen to the brain and its fullest potential, causes major breakdowns. It is known that to combat Alzheimer's and Parkinson's you must keep your mind active you should challenge the mind to learn new things such as a new languages, read on a regular basis. Old minds can learn new tricks, if you continue to try. Health and nutrition and low fat diets are very important. As we spoke in earlier chapters the mind needs oxygen, sugar and blood flow to be healthy. Well if a person eats a high fat diet it is likely their veins are congested with fat and cholesterol. This will in turn restrict the blood flow and cause a less healthy flow of oxygen to the brain. When people grow older they become complacent and unmotivated which will weaken the mind and allow Alzheimer's or Parkinson's to enter.

My grandfather was 85 years old. He was born in Italy and came to the USA in his twenties. He never learned to speak English, but he was very active. At 84 years old he would get up early in the morning walk to the Italian store, purchase the Italian newspaper, pick up some pastry, and walk about five blocks to bring our family the pastry then go back to his house. During the day he would work with his garden and do his chores. Soon after my aunts, uncle and father were unable to continue to care for him. They placed him in an old age home. Within six months he had lost his mind. He did not know who we were, he had no memory and the doctors said he had hardening of the arteries. I think he had Alzheimer's. Think about it - he no longer read the Italian newspaper, he no longer took his walks, and he was restricted to staying in his room. His mind stopped working when he stopped walking which was a form of exercise, and his positive attitude in life was diminished because of where he was now living. He died at 86.

What is Alzheimer's?

Just like the rest of our bodies, our brains change as we age. Most of us notice some slowed thinking and occasional problems remembering and retaining. However, serious memory loss, confusion and other major changes in the way our minds work are not a normal part of aging. They may be a sign that brain cells are failing.

As I explained in the first chapter the brain has 100 billion nerve cells, called neurons. Each nerve cell communicates with many others to form networks.

Nerve cell networks have special jobs. Some are involved in thinking, learning and remembering. Others help us see, hear and smell. Still others tell our muscles when to move.

To do their work, brain cells operate like tiny factories. They take in supplies, generate energy, construct equipment and get rid of waste. Brain cells also process and store information. Keeping everything running requires coordination as well as large amounts of fuel and oxygen.

In Alzheimer's disease, parts of the cell's factory stop running well. Scientists are not sure exactly where the trouble starts. But just like a real factory, backups and breakdowns in one system cause problems in other areas. As damage spreads, cells lose their ability to do their jobs well. Eventually, they die.

What is Parkinson's disease?

Parkinson's disease is a degenerative disorder of the central nervous system which belongs to a group of conditions called motor system disorders, which are the result of the loss of brain cells. The four primary symptoms of Parkinson's Disease are tremor, or trembling in hands, arms, legs, jaw, and face; rigidity, or stiffness of the limbs and trunk, or slowness of movement; and postural instability, or impaired balance and coordination. As these symptoms become more pronounced, patients may have difficulty walking, talking, or completing other simple tasks. Parkinson's disease usually affects people over the age of 50. Parkinson's disease is a brain disorder similar to Alzheimer's it attacks the brain of elderly people. There is no cure for either of these diseases however a healthy brain is less likely to become victim to these disorders.

Many scientists and doctors are now suggesting that people take on new challenges as they get older, this is the best thing people can do to slow down the progression of Alzheimer's and Parkinson's. They recommend learning a new language or being involved in learning dance, Yoga, Tai Chi or other activities which work on memorization and mental focus of the brain. It seems like when we stop pushing the mind it then goes in reverse and the cells begin to dissolve.

CHAPTER THIRTEEN

Nutrition and the Brain

Nutrition and the Brain

You heard the old saying you are what you eat. Well this holds true with the brain and Mind Power. As I explained previously if we thought of the Human as an automobile the body would be all the working parts such as the tires, wheels, engine, etc. The brain would be the driver. Well we can have a great driver but if the vehicle is in bad shape the driver will not be able to drive. The body is the vehicle for our brain so the better it works the better the brain will work. Eating healthy and maintaining a healthy body is essential to having a powerful and successful mind capable of developing Mind Power. The brain needs high levels of oxygen and balanced nutrition for it to work at its highest capacity.

The brain is supplied nutrition from the blood so the healthier the blood is the better it will feed the brain. If your blood is filled with cholesterol and fat it will not have the proper nutrition for the brain. Oxygen must flow to the brain however if the body is unhealthy the oxygen levels will be less so the food for the brain will not be what it needs to be. Healthy blood is produced by eating good foods high in fibers such as fruits, nuts, vegetables and grains. Natural foods produce the best nutrition for the brain.

Foods cooked in fatty acids and fried foods are very bad for the body these foods produce blood filled with fat and cholesterol. Blood filled with fat will not flow properly through the arteries and veins the blood gets restricted and the pressure is affected. Eating foods low in fats and high in fibers should be the target for developing a healthy brain. Eating foods high in protein is also important for the brain. Protein helps the body to stay strong and helps it to rebuild when needed.

While there are many examples of people who live for more then 100 years with little evidence of a decline in brain function, many others are not so fortunate and experience brain disorders as they age, such as Alzheimer disease or Parkinson disease. Although there are many genetic factors that may determine the risk for brain disorders to be considered, many current findings suggest that dietary factors play major roles in determining whether the brain ages successfully or experiences a brain disorder. Dietary factors that interact with disease-causing or predisposing genes in the blood and brain promote the destruction of neurons in the brain. Several studies suggest that high-calorie diets increase the risk for Alzheimer disease and

Parkinson disease. These new studies show that there are direct links between unhealthy diet and brain disorders.

Nutrition for the brain

Increase Water Intake

Since your brain is about eighty percent liquid it is important that you have an adequate supply of water in your diet for your brain to be healthy. Hydrate your brain by consuming at least 84 ounces of water each day. If your body is dehydrated it will increase stress hormones which may damage your brain cells.

Foods for the Brain

One of the best foods for the brain is foods rich in DHA Omega-3 fatty acids which are found in fish and fish oils. DHA Omega-3 is found in the large gray matter of your brain. The gray matter in your brain reproduces cell membranes which plays an important role in the cell function. Neurons of the brain are also rich in Omega-3 fatty acids. It has also been documented that high levels of DHA and Omega-3 fatty acids in the brain will aid in the balance of mood problems, emotional problems and depression.

Antioxidants Great for the Brain

Many researchers have indicated that diets rich in Antioxidants from vegetables and fruits reduce the risk of developing cognitive impairment. This will decrease the deterioration of the brain with age. In the brain the cells convert oxygen to energy and this energy is called free radicals. Free radicals work to rid the body of harmful toxins which promotes a healthy brain and body. Vitamin E and C will inhibit the production of free radicals. These fruits and vegetables are high in Antioxidants and should be in your diet on a daily basis. Cranberries, Blueberries, Blackberries, Strawberries, Raspberries,

Good Eating Habits for the Brain

Many studies of animals and humans have shown that calorie restricted diets are essential for a healthy brain and long life. A calorie restricted diet basically means if you eat less you will live longer and have a healthier brain. Eating foods lower in calories will assist in weight control, healthier organs and a much stronger body. Obesity is known to contribute in Heart attacks, Strokes, Cancer, serous illnesses and disease. It is important that you educate yourself about the foods you eat and develop a good understanding of the calorie amounts of the foods that you consume.

Balance of Protein, Carbohydrates and Fats

The proper balance of protein, carbohydrates and healthy fats for a healthy Brain is fifty percent protein, thirty percent carbohydrates and twenty percent healthy fats. A healthy diet will be low in refined sugars and also high in fiber. Eating protein at each meal assists in the balance of blood sugar levels. Eating lean meats, eggs, cheese, soy, or nuts will limit the absorption of carbohydrates and prevents brain black outs or brain freeze.

The American Cancer Society recommends five to nine servings a day of fruits and vegetables. Remember the more colorful the food the better it is for you. Strive to eat red foods such as strawberries, raspberries, cherries, red peppers and tomatoes, yellow foods such as squash, yellow peppers, bananas and peaches, blue foods such as blueberries, purple foods like plums, orange foods oranges, tangerines and yams, green foods peas, spinach and broccoli.

For a Healthy Brain Diet choose your daily foods from these food groups

Healthy Lean Proteins

Fish	Salmon, Tuna, Mackerel and Herring
Poultry	Skinless Chicken and Turkey
Meats	Lean Beef and Pork
Eggs	Enriched Eggs
Tofu Products	
Soy Products	
Dairy Products	Low Fat Cheese, Cottage Cheese, Low Fat Sugar Free Yogurt and Skim Milk
Beans	Garbanzo and Lentils
Nuts	Walnuts
Seed	Raw unsalted

Healthy Complex Carbohydrates

Berries	Strawberries, Blueberries, Raspberries and Blackberries
Oranges	
Lemons	
Limes	
Grapefruits	
Cherries	

Plums
Broccoli
Brussels Sprouts
Oats
Whole Wheat Products
Wheat Germ
Peppers   Red or Yellow
Pumpkin Squash
Spinach
Tomatoes
Yams
Beans

Healthy Good Fats
Extra Virgin Olive Oil
Avocados
Olives
Salmon
Nuts

We have an old saying in the Martial Arts, "A strong mind develops a strong body and a strong body develops strong mind". The mind and body must interact as one. You cannot be healthy mentally without being healthy physically. Your mind cannot reach its potential without a healthy body. To develop true Mind Power you must maintain a strong healthy body. The only way to develop a strong healthy body is through exercise and healthy eating.

Healthy Eating Develops a Healthy Brain

CHAPTER FOURTEEN

PHYSICAL FITNESS FOR MIND POWER

Physical Fitness for Mind Power

As I explained earlier, physical exercise is very important in the development of mind power. Exercise makes the body strong and a strong body will help in the development of a strong mind. Physical exercise also enhances the amount of oxygen in the blood. The brain is an organ and it is housed in the body, so if the body is ill the brain will also have ill effects. When the body is healthy and strong it allows the brain to be healthy and strong. Exercises which promote cardiovascular effects are the most beneficial to the brain. Cardio exercising will develop healthy blood and the blood is what carries nutrition to the brain. Through cardio exercising blood sugar levels are maintained and the blood will carry higher levels of oxygen. It is known that oxygen and sugar are the food of the brain.

Cardio exercises are exercises which raise the heart beat to over 110 beats per minute. These Cardio exercises should be done for a minimum of twenty to thirty minutes a day, four or five times a week for best results. Cardio exercises are walking or running on a treadmill, exercising on stationary bike, power walking, jogging or any other exercise machine which you do continuous exercises. Martial arts, dance, boxing or aerobics are all good Cardio exercises. You should be involved in a regular exercise program which promotes a cardio workout.

The body needs exercise or it will become weak and sickly. Exercise will develop strong organs which will enhance good health and long life. The long-term importance of physical exercise is essential for a healthy strong brain which functions at a high level. It is known that in general, exercise improves the heart's ability to pump blood more effectively, as well as increases the blood's oxygen-carrying capacity. It is thought that one of the reasons why the elderly, especially those with coronary artery disease or hypertension, tend to suffer some degree of cognitive decline is in part due to a reduction in blood flow to the brain.

As the human ages, exercise should be maintained to prevent mental breakdown or cognitive decline. Researchers have seen selective cognitive benefits which accompany improvement from aerobic fitness. These improvements were clearly attributable to the aerobics workout. Even beyond age 70, cardiovascular exercise can improve memory and reasoning skills. "People who have chosen a lifetime of relative inactivity can benefit mentally from improved aerobic fitness. It's never too late to start; studies show.

A recent study of an elderly group, comparing aerobic exercise to medication showed strong results. Before enrolling in the trial, and four months later, the cognitive abilities of the participants were tested in four areas: memory, executive functioning, attention concentration, and psychomotor speed.

Compared to the medication group, the exercisers showed significant improvements in the higher mental processes of memory and in "executive functions" that involve planning, organization, and the ability to mentally juggle different intellectual tasks at the same time.

What was found was so fascinating, that exercise had its beneficial effect in specific areas of cognitive function that are rooted in the frontal and prefrontal regions of the brain. "The implications are that exercise might be able to offset some of the mental declines that we often associate with the aging process."

Try this great morning wake up exercise for your brain. While you're still in laying in bed, slowly begin to move your toes, move them any way that feels good. Wriggle them, scrunch them, and stretch them. Move all your toes up and down several times, or work just your big toes. Wiggling your toes activates nerves that stimulate your brain and internal organs. Try doing this exercise first thing each morning or after sitting for an extended period of time. It will help you to wake-up and become alert more quickly. Your whole body may feel pleasantly energized. After giving your toes a workout stand up and do some breathing exercises this will send some fresh oxygen to your brain and wake it up.

If you are unable to participate in a regular cardio workout program just take walks. Yes walking has many positive effects on your brain and it is also good for your health. Walking is especially good for your brain, because it increases blood circulation and the oxygen and glucose that reach your brain. Walking is not strenuous, so your leg muscles don't take up extra oxygen and glucose like they do during other forms of exercise. As you walk, you effectively oxygenate your brain. Maybe, this is why, walking can "clear your head" and help you to think better. Movement and exercise increase breathing and heart rate so that more blood flows to the brain, enhancing energy production and waste removal. Studies show that in response to exercise, cerebral blood vessels can grow, even in middle-aged sedentary animals.

Master Dominick A Giacobbe

    In conclusion exercise is very important for a healthy brain. Doing a cardio workout or just walking on a regular basis will enhance your brain functions and decrease the possibility of cognitive decline as you age. Exercise is important as your grow old to keep your brain young.

CHAPTER FIFTEEN

CONCLUSION

CONCLUSION

In conclusion, it will not be easy to develop Mind Power but it is obtainable if you desire to develop it. All good things in life do not come easy. You must work hard for what you want in life. The mind is the greatest tool in the universe. There is no computer or machine that can do all that the brain does. The brain keeps us alive and works every part of our body. The mind gives us the ability to think, feel, speak, walk, have emotions, imagine and dream. Mind Power gives us the power to go beyond the ordinary. It gives us the sixth sense or the third eye in life. Mind Power is developed through meditation, special breathing exercises, positive thinking, having the ability to relax, regular cardio exercise routine and concentration on memory and continued mental challenges which forces you to think. The mind needs to be challenged and worked to be strong. Mind Power is a strong mind working to its fullest potential.

There is an old story that teaches us that we must jump out of our conscious or present world to experience the subconscious world. The story is about a frog that lived in a well. There was a frog that lived in a well. He was very happy he had food, water and all his needs for life. In the well was several other frogs but they were all old. He was the only young frog. One of the old frogs approached the young frog and told him he should jump from the well because there was a better world outside of the well. The young frog thought his suggestion was not good because in the well the frog was comfortable he had his food and felt safe in his life. Each day the old frog would suggest for the young frog to jump from the well and each day he would tell him he was happy and content. One day there was a huge storm, it rained and rained. The well filled to the rim with water. When the young frog wasn't looking, the old frog bit him on the leg. The young frog jumped and went right out of the well. He was amazed there was a beautiful world out there. He saw trees, grass, flowers and life which he never experienced before. There were other young frogs playing and having fun. There was plenty of food and a much better life. He was so happy he jumped away playing with the other frogs.

The story teaches us that we become comfortable with our life style and not eager to make changes in our life. However, we must make changes to find new horizons. Mind Power is a change of your thoughts and actions but like the frog, when you jump from your present world and into the world of Mind Power you will have new experiences which will lead you to a better and stronger life. Our thoughts are controlled by our mind, so make strong positive thoughts and trust in Mind Power. Jump out of your well and leave the world of the present and experience the world of a Mind Master.

Mind Power is developed through discipline and determination. Instill a regular exercise routine in your daily life and stick with it. Discipline yourself to do the breathing exercises, everyday. Challenge your mind with concentration and memory exercises. However, the most important exercise for Mind Power is meditation. Although all the different lessons in this book will lead you to Mind Power, it is the meditation which is most important. Be determined in your meditation; keep working at it until you succeed. Be positive in your thoughts and in your actions. Do not allow negativity to be present in your mind. Be strong in your actions and show confidence. Keep your mind calm and well balanced. Practice peace of mind and understanding. Be patient and possess a never quit attitude. Have courage and always show honor. Respect your mind and respect your body. Be safe in your actions and confident in your decisions. You are what you think you are. Look beyond the horizon and all your dreams will come true. You have the MIND now develop the POWER!

"BE STRONG, NEVER QUIT AND BELIEVE"
MASTER YOUR MIND!
DEVELOP MIND POWER!
BECOME A MIND MASTER!

Experience Grand Master Giacobbe's Amazing live Seminar on Mind Power

It will be a life changing experience!

Grand Master Dominick Giacobbe is a true mind master. He is well respected around the world for his abilities in Mind development. He has been conducting seminars for the past 20 years on the development of the mind. He conducts amazing seminars in the development of Mind Power, which consists of teaching positive thinking, breathing exercises and meditation. His seminars are motivating and will inspire you to develop your mind. He conducts seminars teaching the traditional art of Tang Soo Do, Korean Karate and physical fitness. Grand Master Giacobbe

Master Dominick A Giacobbe

also teaches seminars for developing and learning the ancient Military Yoga exercises called Ti Ji Nae Bu, these Yoga exercises are great for stress release, physical fitness, enhancing Chi energy and the development of harmony with the universe. Seminars can be arranged for your group or sports team by emailing Master Giacobbe at tangsoo8@comcast.net or call (856) 627-2323.

Master Dominick A. Giacobbe known as the "MIND MASTER" is a true Grand Master of the 2,000 year old art of Tang Soo Do, Korean Karate. Internationally known as a Mind Master, Giacobbe has been viewed by millions on the "GUINNESS WORLD RECORDS" international TV show. He was labeled on the show and in the Guinness World's Record Book as the "MIND WARRIOR", for his amazing performance of Mind over Matter. He has performed his feats of Mind over Matter hundreds of times on numerous TV programs, in magazines and at live appearances.

Grand Master Dominick A. Giacobbe the holder of an 8th Dan Black belt in the 2,000 year old art of Tang Soo Do, Korean Karate, began his studies of Karate in 1968 under Grand Master J C Shin, who is well known for teaching Karate movie star Chuck Norris. Master Shin personally trained Mr. Giacobbe.

In the late 60's and early 70's, Master Giacobbe gained a reputation as a top tournament competitor on the East Coast. Master Giacobbe also received special Tang Soo Do training for several years with Grand Master H C Hwang, son of the founder of Tang Soo Do and with Grand Master C S Kim, world famous Tang Soo Do champion. In 1974, Master Giacobbe opened the Tang Soo Karate Academy in Blackwood, New Jersey. His Academy now in Pine Hill, New Jersey is one of the largest Karate schools in the USA. In 1977 he traveled to Korea to fine tune his Art and learned the ancient techniques of Mind Power, derived from the internal Chi energy.

His skills in developing mind power through meditation and special breathing exercises has set him apart from all other Martial Artist. Master Giacobbe has appeared numerous times on TV demonstrating his unbelievable demonstrations of Tang Soo Do Mind Power, in which he pierces his arms with sharpened motorcycle spokes, hangs buckets of water and demonstrates this with no blood and no pain. He amazed audiences on Guinness World Records, Incredible Sunday, That's Incredible, Evening Magazine, Good Morning America, Sally Jessie Raphael, CNN, After Hours, Entertainment Tonight, and several other National TV Shows.

His expertise has been used for the training of many professional athletes. In 1980, members of the Philadelphia Eagle Football team began training with Master Giacobbe to enhance their skills in Football. In 1987, Coach Buddy Ryan assigned the entire Philadelphia Eagle defense to train off-season with Master Giacobbe.

For five years the Eagle defense was the best in the league. Mr. Giacobbe personally trained NFL stars Reggie White and Mike Quick. He was also the special physical trainer for many World Champion Boxers, working on 15 World Championship Bouts. Master Giacobbe personally trained Evander Holyfield, Pernell Whitaker and Sugar Ray Leonard for several of their Championship fights. Master Giacobbe has also appeared on the covers of 6 Martial Arts Magazines including Black Belt Magazine and Karate Kung Fu Illustrated. His expertise in Karate has been the subject of many international magazine stories. In 1985, he won a Gold Medal in Japan at the World Super People festival. Master Giacobbe amazed the Japanese judges standing atop authentic razor sharp Japanese Samurai swords without getting cut.

The Governor of New Jersey has also awarded Master Giacobbe for his Juvenile Offender Program. The program took troubled juveniles and put them in Karate training where all of the kids had positive results. In 1983, Master Giacobbe was presented the Excalibur Award from the American Cancer Society for his donation of over $600,000.00 from the Fight for Cancer National Karate Championships, which he sponsors in Atlantic City annually.

In the year 2000, Master Giacobbe was inducted into Black Belt Magazine Hall of Fame. This is the highest honor a Martial Artist can achieve. He shares this honor with Bruce Lee, Jackie Chan and Chuck Norris. Master Dominick A. Giacobbe was inducted in as Man of the Year, 2000.

Printed in Great Britain
by Amazon.co.uk, Ltd.,
Marston Gate.